FACTOLOGY
ROBOTS & AI

Artificial intelligence revolution

Open up a world of information!

ARE YOU READY TO EXPLORE...

We're at the beginning of a robotics revolution! Awesome AI is already greeting us each morning when we unlock our phones, figuring out what we want on our feeds, powering Google and Alexa, showing us the way on map apps and helping us keep track of our cash. As we speak, millions of robots are working in factories around the world, assembling cars, sorting stock and packing products. Before long they'll be helping doctors diagnose diseases, driving you to school and delivering your shopping.

In the future, smart robot swarms could be sent to sweep up oil spills, and chips implanted in your brain may let you move a computer mouse using your mind! Drones and droids, chatbots and chorebots, cyborgs and softbots – it's the dawning of a dazzling digital age!

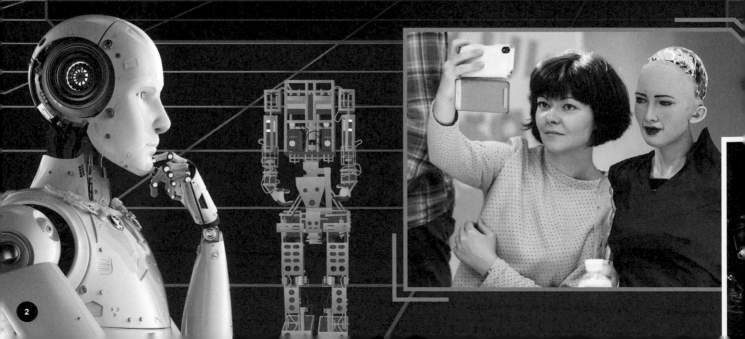

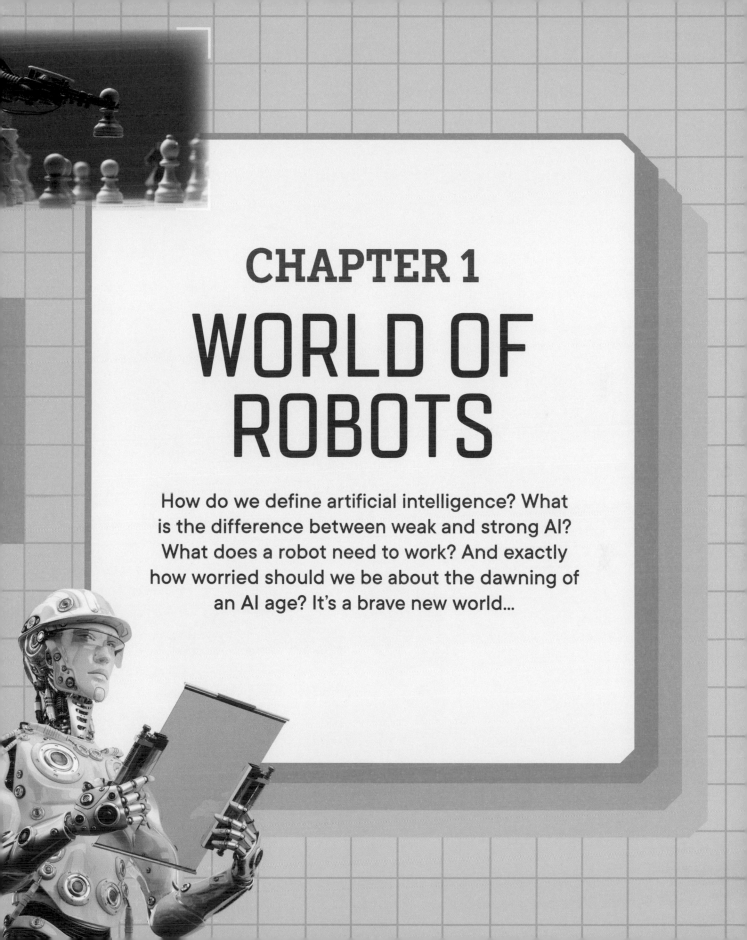

CHAPTER 1

WORLD OF ROBOTS

How do we define artificial intelligence? What is the difference between weak and strong AI? What does a robot need to work? And exactly how worried should we be about the dawning of an AI age? It's a brave new world...

WHAT IS A ROBOT?

When you hear the word robot, what do you think of? Is it a human-like metal machine? That's probably the same for most people, but in reality there are LOTS of different types of robots...

There are so many different kinds of robots, from smart vacuum cleaners to rovers on Mars, how do you decide what one actually is?

Most experts agree that robots are computer-controlled machines able to carry out a series of tasks on their own. Some are operated remotely, while others can be programmed in advance. Some have moving limbs, like mechanical legs or arms, while others can fly. Some build cars in factories, while others help doctors perform operations. But all robots have certain similarities in the way that they work...

SENSE

Robots use sensors, such as lasers, cameras or motion detectors, to gather information about their body or the environment. They might use them to hear instructions, feel their movements, see an object ahead or measure changes in light. This information helps them to make decisions about what to do next.

THINK

Robots have a programmable brain (usually a computer) that processes the sensory information and tells its parts what to do, just like your brain tells your muscles to move.

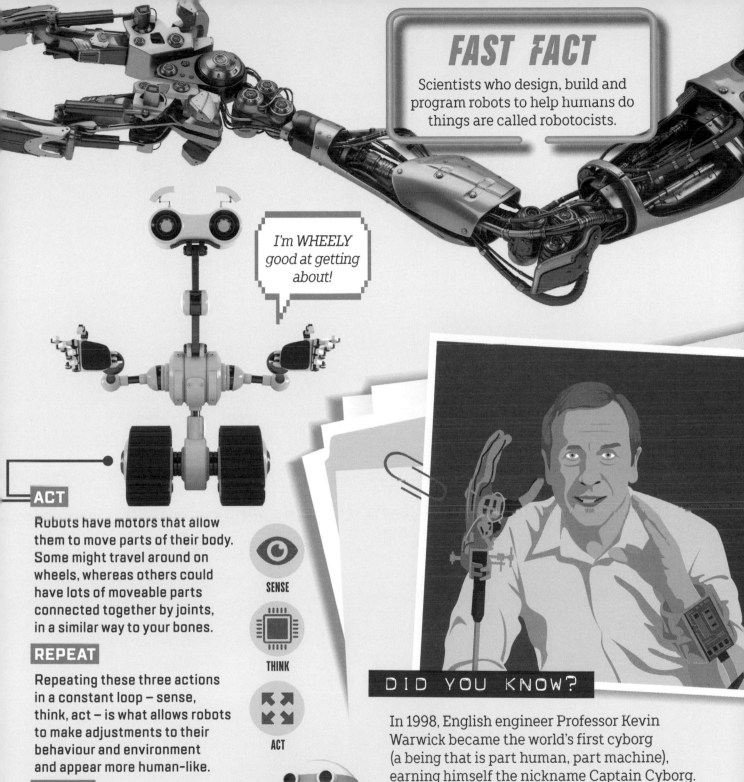

FAST FACT

Scientists who design, build and program robots to help humans do things are called robotocists.

I'm WHEELY good at getting about!

ACT

Robots have motors that allow them to move parts of their body. Some might travel around on wheels, whereas others could have lots of moveable parts connected together by joints, in a similar way to your bones.

SENSE

THINK

ACT

REPEAT

Repeating these three actions in a constant loop – sense, think, act – is what allows robots to make adjustments to their behaviour and environment and appear more human-like.

POWER

Robots need power to do all these things, in the same way you need energy from food to move. Most get this from electricity, either from batteries or being plugged in.

DID YOU KNOW?

In 1998, English engineer Professor Kevin Warwick became the world's first cyborg (a being that is part human, part machine), earning himself the nickname Captain Cyborg. A microchip implanted in his wrist allowed him to control lights, door locks and heaters via an electronic signal. When scientists in New York used the chip to link Warwick's nervous system to the internet, he was able to make a robotic arm in the UK mimic his movements!

WHAT IS ARTIFICIAL INTELLIGENCE?

Artificial intelligence, or AI for short, is a computer system that can do things in a human-like way. But getting computers to act and think like us isn't easy!

What is intelligence, anyway?

Scientists who work in AI are trying to build computers that act in a similar way to humans. To do this well, first they need to figure out what human intelligence is and how people think. This can be tricky, because the way we think is very complicated indeed!

HOW DO WE USE AI?

- AI computers can act as the 'brain' for a human or animal-like robot.

- AI can also be a program that runs on a phone or computer, such as Siri or Alexa.

TYPES OF AI

1 WEAK (NARROW) AI

This is the type of AI that exists at the moment and that lots of us use everyday. It's used to carry out a single task, and do it really well. In fact, it may do it better than humans!

Examples

1 **DEEP BLUE** A good example of Weak AI is a computer that can play chess. In 1997, a super-computer called Deep Blue beat world champion chess player Garry Kasparov. Deep Blue was an AI system that had been programmed with the rules and strategies of the game. It followed the instructions that had been coded into it and this allowed it to make moves more quickly and precisely than grandmaster Garry. Deep Blue wasn't more intelligent than Garry, but it was very good at playing chess!

2 **RECOMMEND TAGS** Websites or applications that work out your likes and dislikes and then offer recommendations (such as Netflix or YouTube) are Weak AI.

3 **DIGITAL VOICE ASSISTANTS** Using voice recognition and natural language processing, virtual assistants such as Siri and Alexa analyse data and respond to queries.

4 **SEARCH ENGINES** Google and other search engines are also examples of Weak AI.

2 STRONG (GENERAL) AI

This is the type of AI that we may have in the future. It would be able to act and think just like a human, carrying out different types of tasks on its own. Weak AI can look at large amounts of information and use it to make a decision, but that's different to understanding a problem in the same way as a human. Right now, we're still a long way off from developing technology that can mimic abilities such as understanding and recognising imagination and emotion.

Sci-fi examples

1 **HAL 9000** in *2001: A Space Odyssey*
2 **WALL-E**
3 **R2-D2** from *Star Wars*

3 SUPER AI

Super AI would be better at thinking than humans in every way. At the moment it's just a theory (and the stuff of science fiction!) but the idea is that once an AI system becomes able to learn from itself, this would quickly snowball...

1 The AI system might start off with a human-level intelligence.

2 As it learns from itself it wouldn't be long before it achieved genius-level intelligence.

3 Now it's learning at genius-level, it would get smarter and smarter...

4 ...until its intelligence exploded, creating a superintelligence!

MIND GAMES

AI systems are getting better at 'learning' in a similar way to humans

HOW DOES AI LEARN?

Historically, computers have done things by following a set of instructions that a human has programmed into it, step by step. Now, advances in technology mean that AI systems have the ability to learn and adapt as they make decisions, without much help from humans! They do this using a technology called machine learning. Today when someone talks about AI, this is usually what they're referring to.

WHAT IS MACHINE LEARNING?

2 A little time later, you see another animal. It looks like this.
You're told this is also a cat. You look at it closely. You remember being told about cats before.

3 Some more time passes, then you see this animal.
This time you know right away it's a cat. You've worked it out by noticing patterns (each animal has a similar body shape, whiskers, a tail, pointy ears) across a number of experiences.

1 Imagine you're a baby and you see an animal that looks like this.
You don't know what it is, but you're told it's a cat. You've never heard that word before, so you might remember it, or you might not.

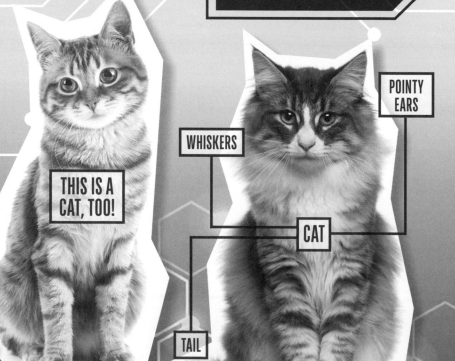

THIS IS CALLED A CAT

THIS IS A CAT, TOO!

POINTY EARS

WHISKERS

CAT

TAIL

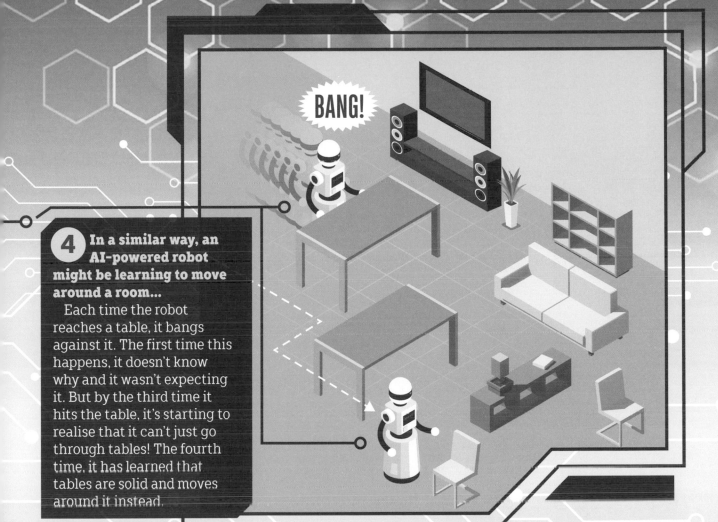

BANG!

4 **In a similar way, an AI-powered robot might be learning to move around a room...**

Each time the robot reaches a table, it bangs against it. The first time this happens, it doesn't know why and it wasn't expecting it. But by the third time it hits the table, it's starting to realise that it can't just go through tables! The fourth time, it has learned that tables are solid and moves around it instead.

Watch this SPACE

Scientists searching space for signals from aliens think **machine learning** could help them! That's because looking for extraterrestrial life is essentially a data-sorting exercise.

Using some of the world's biggest telescopes, alien-hunters listen out for radio signals that change in a particular way. But the telescopes pick up so many signals (often from human

and Earth technology) it can be tough to filter out the ones they're after. Machine learning is able to comb through the millions of signals emitted and pinpoint any that are unexpected. Out of this world, eh?

The James Webb Space Telescope launched in December 2021

HUMANS!

We see robots in movies that have their own thoughts and ideas all the time, but how would we know if a robot was really as clever as a human?

THE TURING TEST

In 1950 a British mathematician named Alan Turing came up with a test to answer this question. The Turing test, as it's known, is a game with three players – a human judge, a human contestant and a machine contestant. The judge sits at a desk apart from the contestants and has to decide which is which by asking them questions on a computer.

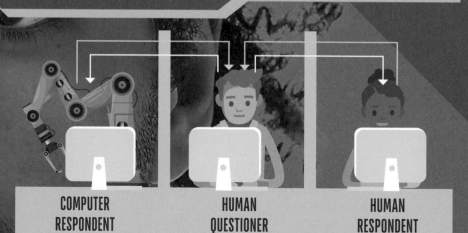

COMPUTER RESPONDENT

HUMAN QUESTIONER

HUMAN RESPONDENT

During the test, the judge asks the contestants questions about a specific subject. After a set amount of time, the judge has to decide which contestant is human and which is a machine. The test is repeated lots of times. If the machine can trick the judge into thinking it's a real person in half or more of the tests, then it's said to have intelligence.

Turing said that by the year 2000 a computer 'would be able to play the imitation game so well that an average interrogator will not have more than a 70% chance of making the right identification (machine or human) after five minutes of questioning.' But so far no computer has passed the test.

HANG ON A SEC...

The test is brilliant in its simplicity, but critics say there are a couple of problems with it.

1 The test doesn't actually measure intelligence. It tests how much a machine can behave like a human. What if a machine solved a really hard maths problem that humans couldn't? It would have acted in an intelligent way but still failed the test.

2 An inexperienced judge might miss something important in the contestants' answers.

There's one thing that Turing didn't make clear about his test. Should the judge always know beforehand that one of the contestants is a machine?

ROBOTS

CHINESE ROOM ARGUMENT

In 1980, American philosopher John Searle argued that the Turing test couldn't be used to decide whether a machine was as intelligent as a human, and he came up with a thought experiment (a way of using your imagination to explore tricky ideas) to try and prove it.

Searle (who can't understand Chinese) imagined himself in a room with a pile of Chinese characters and an instruction book.

If a computer is simply following instructions, is it really thinking? What about when you write something in a book at school – aren't you just following a set of instructions?

He then pictured a Chinese speaker outside the room posting him questions written in Chinese through a door. After looking up the answer in his instruction book, Searle pushes the correct Chinese characters back through the door. To the Chinese speaker, it seems as though the person in the room understands Chinese, even though he doesn't.

Searle argued that this is exactly what an AI machine would be doing during the Turing test – choosing the correct symbols without any real understanding of what they meant.

FAST⚡FACT

The **CAPTCHA** test used on websites as security is the Turing test in reverse – humans try to convince a computer that they aren't a computer!

ALGORITHMS MADE EASY

This example will help you wrap your brain around how algorithms work...

GOAL   Make a smoothie

STEPS

1 Add fruit to the blender

2 Add milk to the blender

3 Put the lid on the blender

4 Switch on the blender

SUCCESS:

By following these precise instructions in the exact order laid out, you will end up with a yummy smoothie. But what if you did step 4 after steps 1&2? There would be a mess all over the counter that you'd quickly have to clean up! It's the same with computer algorithms.

LET'S CODE:

While you understand this 'algorithm', it's gobbledygook to a computer until you translate it into code – the language used in all programming.

```
0000101100111
01011101011101
0110101010001
```

AWESOME ALGORITHMS

See
Machine vision powers self-driving cars and face identification for police work and banking/payment portals.

Hear
Gunshots are picked up by AI, analysed, and the relevant agencies alerted!

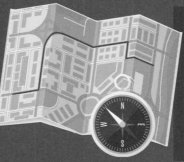

Speak
Google Maps and Sat Nav technology revolutionised the old-school practice of stopping every few minutes to check a paper map. The days of getting lost are well and truly over (bar a few tech 'blips')!

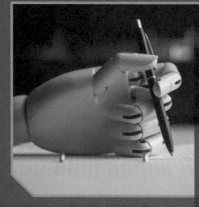

Write
Important news organisations such as *The New York Times* are using AI to report on world events. And in 2016, a Japanese AI 'author' co-created *The Day A Computer Writes A Novel*, which made it onto a literary prize list!

Just like your body needs your brain to tell it what to do, AI wouldn't exist without algorithms. In its simplest form, an algorithm is a sequence or set of rules to complete a task or solve a problem. But how are they put to use?

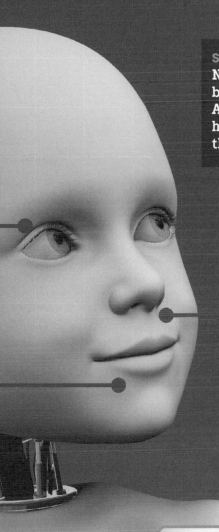

Smell
New fragrances are being created by clever AI that can anticipate how much we will love their smell!

Touch
A supermarket robot can pick raspberries that are ready to eat, using sensors and cameras. It will be able to pop over 7,000 of the fruit into a basket in one day!

THE BIG THREE
There are three main AI algorithm categories

1 SUPERVISED LEARNING
Like a student being taught by a teacher, the algorithm is given some clearly labelled data, which it uses to grow and learn. It can then predict outcomes for other data.

For example, we give a computer some pictures of different cats and we teach it that they all share the same label – CAT.

LABEL 'CAT'

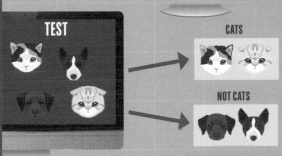

TEST

CATS

NOT CATS

Then we test the computer by showing it pictures of cats and dogs. It has 'learned' what a cat is, and what isn't.

2 UNSUPERVISED LEARNING
This time there's no 'teacher'. The data is simply given to the algorithm without any labels. The algorithm looks for patterns in the data and groups them together without any help.

NO LABELS

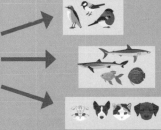

3 REINFORCED LEARNING
This is when the algorithm gets either rewards or penalties for the actions it performs. In the same way that you might get an ice cream for being helpful but be sent to your room for spitting food, the algorithm gets rewards for correct actions, and penalties for wrong ones. The algorithm explores its environment, performs actions and learns from the feedback.

WILL ROBOTS TAKE YOUR JOB?

Doctor, musician, athlete or pilot... are you still deciding which career to pick in the future? Whatever you choose, AI is predicted to create 97 million new jobs around the globe by 2025, so not all of your 'colleagues' may be human!

1.7 million

The number of manufacturing jobs already replaced by robots and automation systems since 2020. But more roles will need to be filled – 'armies' of AI researchers for example, who must keep up with new tech.

Who's the boss?

It's possible that you won't just be working alongside AI programmes – you could be hired by one, as well! Research shows that many companies are using AI to analyse CVs submitted by potential employees to save time in deciding who to invite for an interview.

Rev up!

Check out our special traffic light system to find out where your dream job falls in the near future. Is it time to rethink your plans?

PIPPED AT THE POST!

- Assembly line and manufacturing workers
- Customer service
- Taxi and bus drivers (90% of long-haul truckers may be replaced by self-driving technology)
- Accountants/insurance underwriters (clever computer algorithms can come up with formulas in seconds)
- Market research and data entry
- Security guards

BETTER BE QUICK!

- Forensic scientists
- Couriers
- Radiologists
- Soldiers
- Cashiers in supermarkets and other kinds of shops
- Dieticians
- Web developers
- Receptionists (Pepper the humanoid robot can already greet and respond to guests)

HUMANS ONLY (FOR NOW!)

- Teachers
- Human resource managers
- Therapists
- Singers
- Social workers
- Lawyers and judges
- Managers and directors
- AI training engineers
- Athletes
- Plumbers, electricians and other 'trade' roles

99% The accuracy of one AI program in detecting breast cancer – that's as high as many world-renowned experts!

77 The number of chemicals that could stop the spread of COVID, identified by a supercomputer.

Man versus machine

Some people are worried that AI and robotics are powerful enough to edge out the human touch, but that's simply not the case! Weak spots include:
* **Using common sense** to make moral and social decisions.

* **A lack of empathy** – even the most sophisticated technology can't 'feel' someone else's emotions.
* Movements that demand **hand–eye coordination**, such as sports.
* **Navigating unknown** and unstructured spaces.

No sick days

A big plus point for companies is that robots never feel under the weather and take time off to recover. Since 2020, many of our automated friends have been able to detect 'pain' – a sign they're damaged – and repair themselves!

GREAT WORK, PERKINS!

You've got this!

Mankind has always pushed itself forward, from the first cave people who sparked a fire two million years ago to the Moon landings in 1969 and the invention of the internet 40 years ago. Change can be scary, but if you embrace it, exciting things can happen.

'AS WITH THE INTERNET, THE REAL GAINS IN JOBS WILL COME FROM PLACES WHERE OUR IMAGINATIONS CANNOT TAKE US YET'

Byron Reese, author of *The Fourth Age* and all-round tech guru

6 HOURS How quickly AI created by Google can design computer chips, winning (virtually) hands down against humans who take months to complete the same task.

Banishing boredom

One bonus of using AI and robots to do repetitive, boring jobs is that it frees up humans to work on more rewarding and fun projects. If you could dream big and do anything you like, where would your imagination take you?

ARE YOU AN
AI NINJA?

SEE IF YOU'VE GOT WHAT IT TAKES TO KEEP UP WITH THE TECHNOLOGICAL TIMES!

- ☑ EMOTIONAL INTELLIGENCE
- ☑ CREATIVITY
- ☑ CRITICAL THINKING AND PROBLEM SOLVING
- ☑ STRONG VERBAL AND WRITTEN COMMUNICATION
- ☑ PEOPLE MANAGEMENT
- ☑ BASIC MATHEMATICS

SHOULD ROBOTS HAVE RIGHTS?

YES

Whoever you are, wherever you live and whatever you do, you have basic rights and freedoms. These are your human rights. They're things like dignity, fairness, equality, respect and independence. Animals have some rights. Companies have some rights. But what about robots? Should they have rights, too?

DEFFO!

☑ The World Economic Forum has predicted that by 2025, robots and machines driven by AI will have taken over 85 million jobs. But they have no worker rights. If they're doing so much work for us, do we have a responsibility to protect them?

☑ Robots are only set to become more advanced. And because they'll learn to become more like humans, they could develop the ability to know right from wrong, to experience emotions and to be self-aware or conscious. If that happens, there's an argument that there should be new laws to protect them.

☑ People already have strong opinions about robots. Some are scared they'll take away human jobs. Others are excited about what they'll bring to the world. That means people could easily discriminate against robots and laws might be needed to make sure they're treated with equality, respect and dignity.

NO WAY!

☒ Some people believe that even if a robot's behaviour is the same as a human's, it will never be a living creature and so shouldn't have the same rights as a human.

☒ At the moment, some robots do jobs that are very dangerous for humans, like disabling bombs. But if robots develop self-awareness they might not want to. And if they have the same rights as humans, it might be unethical for them to do certain jobs, which would arguably defeat the purpose of building them in the first place!

NO

HUMAN RIGHTS

ROBOT RIGHTS

So many questions

If a machine doesn't work properly, it's easy to get cross. You might kick a car if it's not working, or shout at your laptop if it freezes. But what if those machines had feelings? What if it got upset? Or what if it got angry back at you for shouting? Who is responsible? The robot, or the human who programmed it? AI kicks up a lot of questions.

Meet SOPHIA
the trailblazing humanoid robot

In 2016, David Hanson created a very special humanoid. Sophia, as she's called, has a face like a female human. But the back of her head shows all the workings of a robot. She was modelled on ancient Egyptian queen Nefertiti, actress Audrey Hepburn and the inventor's own wife. She can have conversations and shows lots of different human emotions. She's even been interviewed by journalists!

In 2017, Sophia was given citizenship of Saudi Arabia – making her the first robot in the world to be given 'legal personhood' (treated as a person for legal purposes).

Later that year, she was also named the United Nations Development Programme's Innovation Champion, making her the first non-human to be given a United Nations title.

Not everyone is excited about her. Lots of people think that the citizenship was just given to her as a PR stunt.

Sophia with creator David Hanson

And not everyone wants robots to be granted personhood status. Over 285 experts in medicine, robotics, AI and ethics wrote a letter to the European Commission saying that giving robots rights is a bad idea and could damage human rights. What do you think?

Back of Sophia's head showing inner workings

SECRET WEAPON

The possibilities of AI are exciting, but not everyone uses it for the greater good. This powerful tech is also being weaponised, so how do we prevent problems in the future?

TROUBLE ON THE HORIZON

Advances in AI and robotics benefit many industries, but there are also risks. Some people worry about the military using robots which can think for themselves, or oppressive governments misusing AI to spy on people, spread fear and widen their control.

DEADLY DECISIONS

The ability to send a robot on a dangerous mission, while a human controls it remotely back at base, has saved many lives. But it's now possible to create weapons which don't need human control at all. Once they're programmed, these drones, robots, submarines or tanks can independently search for specific targets, then make their own decisions about whether to attack enemy weapons, radars and even people, without any human command. These machines can operate on land, on water, underwater and even in space.

IN THE WRONG HANDS

So far, these weapons have only been used in military operations against objects, with humans ready to step in if anything goes wrong. But powerful technology in the wrong hands is a real worry. Some of the world's most respected scientists and AI entrepreneurs have expressed concerns that dictators, criminals and terrorists could use these machines to threaten, control and even kill.

EYES AND EARS EVERYWHERE

Technology can be used as a weapon against freedom, too. Countries such as China, Iran, North Korea, Syria and Vietnam are widely known for their mass surveillance. By spying on normal citizens, they can gather information to keep their authoritarian governments in power.

It's widely thought that more than half of the world's almost one billion surveillance cameras are located in China. These cameras use AI facial recognition (and possibly capture voice data too) to track people's locations, their behaviour and even who they socialise with. The Chinese government also uses AI technology to control access to the internet, track mobile phones and closely monitor chat and messaging services to build up data about individuals living in China.

FAST⚡FACT

In October 2022, a pro-Russian hacking group disrupted websites belonging to key politicians in Bulgaria and told them it was punishment for betraying Russia and supplying weapons to Ukraine.

ONLINE OUTLAWS

When used for the wrong reasons, the internet can be another powerful and destructive weapon. Terrorist or extremist political groups and criminals can use the web to disrupt systems, make threats and cause fear – this is called cyber terrorism.

By hacking into computers and using AI, these groups can introduce viruses into systems to stop them working, steal data and important information, or hack into websites to stop communication or spread very believable fake news. As AI evolves, this could make it easier for hackers to carry out cyber attacks, meaning they could happen more often and with better accuracy.

LOOKING TO THE FUTURE

As quickly as people are finding new ways to misuse this technology, there are many more experts across the world working together to explore methods to make AI safer in the future and prevent further harm.

Here in the UK, the Office for Artificial Intelligence is working with experts and organisations across the globe, like G7 and UNESCO, to get international and national policies and relations in place so AI is used in safe, lawful and ethical ways.

By working together and sharing knowledge on how to use AI responsibly, we can keep people safe so that everyone can enjoy the awesome potential of AI.

FRIEND OR FOE?

Could AI ever become too clever and threaten humankind?

AI VS AGI

Today we use what is called applied AI - where we program a machine to do a specific job. But researchers are working towards artificial general intelligence (AGI) or advanced AI. This would allow a machine to perform any task an intelligent human could and then improve, learn, make decisions and ultimately think for itself!

TIME TO GET SERIOUS

One theory is that these advanced AI machines might keep learning and improving and eventually become smarter than humans. Would we still be able to control them if that happened? And what if these ultra-smart AI decided that humans were getting in the way of what they wanted to do? It could end quite badly for us!

SKYNET OR SKY'S THE LIMIT?

Although Stuart Russell, a leading expert on AI, believes that AGI will exist within our lifetimes, it certainly hasn't reached this stage yet. So, there's no need to worry about a Terminator-type takeover at the moment. Like John Connor says in *The Terminator*, the future has not been written. We still have time to plan, prepare and work together to get AI tech right so that it can't harm humanity.

POLICE

THEY SAID WHAT?!

Some big thinkers in science, philosophy and AI research have expressed concerns about the dangers AI might pose in the future. They agree that we need to be cautious about the AI technology that we develop, that we need better AI safety regulations and that we must explore solutions to potential dangers before they even arise.

*Success in creating AI would be the biggest event in **human history**. Unfortunately, it might also be the last, unless we learn how to avoid the risks.*
STEPHEN HAWKING

*Machine intelligence is the **last invention** that humanity will ever need to make.*
NICK BOSTROM

*Mark my words. AI is far more **dangerous** than **nuclear warheads**.*
ELON MUSK

THE BRIGHT SIDE
Advanced AI could kickstart a golden age for humans! It could help us find the answer to climate change, end poverty across the world or slow down and even eliminate diseases like cancer. But we need to start thinking now about how we can keep AI systems under control in the future, so AI can only be used for good and the advancement of humankind.

WHAT'S THE BIG IDEA?
Stuart J Russell has suggested building an oracle AI system which is designed to only answer questions. Oracles could tell us whether a particular advanced AI design was safe or not to build, or even how to code AI with human morals and values. Others recommend that all AI are coded with a kill switch. This would restrict the machine's intelligence so humans could stay in control by being able to override the AI's decision making – if needed.

FUTURE THINKING
Organisations across the globe (such as OpenAI, which is committed to reducing any risks that AI might pose) collaborate to deal with global AI challenges and to make sure advanced AI is super safe and will be a benefit to all of humanity.

BATTLING BIAS

From asking Alexa to play your favourite song to YouTube suggesting what video you should watch next, we use AI every day. It's not perfect, though. Unconscious bias is one area we need to improve so that AI can be used without discriminating against some people

WHAT IS UNCONSCIOUS BIAS?

Bias is the thoughts, ideas and beliefs we have about people, places or things, especially when we use these to make an unfair judgement or decision. When we don't realise we're being biased, we call it unconscious bias.

HOW CAN AI BE BIASED?

It's the humans' fault! AI systems learn to make decisions based on the data that we choose to give them. AI learns from the patterns it can see in data, so if there are errors that humans have missed – like data that isn't very diverse or doesn't reflect a group of people fairly – AI starts to reproduce results which highlight these biases.

WHAT ARE THE DANGERS?

Unconscious bias can reinforce issues that we are actively trying to tackle in our societies, like institutional or structural racism, or prejudices about gender, age or background.

For example, facial software recognition recognises whiter faces more easily than those with darker skin tones because white faces were used more often in the training data. That data was unconsciously biased, so now the decisions the AI is producing are biased, too.

UNDER THE RADAR

As these biases enter AI systems unintentionally, errors may not be recognised until they have been programmed into the AI software. At this stage, many people may have already been affected by the decisions made by the AI software.

HERE ARE SOME EXAMPLES...

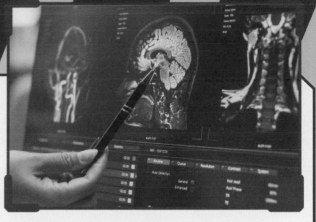

1 AMAZON'S HIRING ALGORITHM

Retail giant Amazon had to stop using the AI system that helped them pick the best people for new jobs, after they realised it was biased against women. Amazon discovered that when women applied for tech jobs, the AI system did not score them fairly.

HOW DID THIS HAPPEN?

This was because Amazon looked at who had applied for their tech jobs in the last 10 years and fed this data into their AI system. As most of the people applying were men, the AI system saw this pattern and taught itself that Amazon preferred men to do these jobs!

2 BIAS IN US HEALTHCARE

An AI system that was used across hospitals in America to decide when people needed healthcare treatment was revealed to be biased against Black patients. This system mostly decided that Black patients had to be more unwell than white patients before they received the same level of care.

HOW DID THIS HAPPEN?

The system was trained using past data which showed that, for many reasons, Black patients tended to spend less than white patients on healthcare. Without considering what individuals could afford, the system had wrongly taught itself that the more you spent on healthcare, the sicker you were.

THERE'S NO (A) I IN TEAM

AI technology is still young – there is plenty we can do to improve it and minimise unconscious bias so that there are equal opportunities for everyone to benefit from AI.

STRENGTH IN DIFFERENCES

To limit bias in AI systems, we need to use data that is as inclusive and diverse as possible. We can achieve this by creating diverse teams (women and men of different ages, from all over the world, with different backgrounds) to program these systems, choose the training data and interpret the final results.

BEST OF BOTH WORLDS

Testing AI systems to discover and then remove any biases is also really important. The 'human-in-the-loop' model gives humans the opportunity to interact with AI to highlight any prejudices that AI systems can't see. When we discover these and fix them, the system then re-learns and improves each time. Now that's teamwork making the dream work!

ASTOUNDING
STORIES
OF SUPER-SCIENCE

THE FIFTH-DIMENSION CATAPULT
A Complete Novelette of an Extraordinary Interdimensional Rescue
BY MURRAY LEINSTER

THE GATE TO XORAN
by Hal K. Wells

CHAPTER 2
RISE OF THE ROBOTS

The idea of an intelligent machine able to carry out humans' wishes has been around for thousands of years, but it's only in the last hundred years that the science of robotics started to come together. Let's take a look at some of the major milestones along the way...

Mythical MACHINES

Robots might seem like a new idea, but humans have been dreaming of creating artificial servants from lifeless materials for thousands of years in their myths and stories

GREEK MYTHS 700BC

STORY OF TALOS

The story goes that Zeus, king of the gods, wanted to protect the island of Crete from invaders. Lucky for him, Hephaestus, another Greek god, was brilliant at inventing stuff and blacksmithing. So, he set about making a giant bronze man, who stomped around the island three times a day and chucked enormous boulders at enemy ships that came too close.

A tube connected his head to one of his feet, and through it ran a mysterious energy that the Greeks called ichor. One ancient story tells how the scary sorceress Medea destroyed Talos. She bewitched him to make him graze his ankle on a sharp rock. The ichor flowed out and Talos fell dead, with a mighty thud.

HEPHAESTUS DOES IT AGAIN!

When the human Prometheus stole fire from the Greek gods, Zeus was furious! He tasked Hephaestus with making a beautiful woman out of clay. She was called Pandora and was brought to life and sent to Earth – along with a jar full of the world's evils. To cause trouble with the humans, Zeus had already programmed her (a bit like a robot) to open the jar and release countless troubles on humanity.

GOLDEN GIRLS

Hephaestus lived on Mount Olympus where he had a massive workshop. It was so big that he even had some one-eyed giants (or cyclopes) working with him. But they weren't enough, so he cleverly decided to make himself some extra beings to help out. Homer described these golden handmaidens in a famous ancient Greek poem called *The Iliad*.

The handmaidens looked just like humans but were made of pure gold.

FACT ANCIENT GREEK POET HESIOD WAS ONE OF THE FIRST TO WRITE ABOUT A ROBOT-LIKE FIGURE IN THE MYTH OF TALOS.

Eighteenth-century painting of Pygmalion and Galatea

BRINGING A SCULPTURE TO LIFE

Yet another tale from ancient Greece (except we hear about this one through the Roman writer, Ovid) tells of the sculptor Pygmalion who carved a woman out of ivory and then fell in love with her. He prayed to Aphrodite, the goddess of love, to bring his sculpture – which he named Galatea – to life. She did. They got married and had a daughter called Paphos, who gave her name to the city in Cyprus devoted to Aphrodite.

GOLEMS

A golem isn't only a type of Pokémon! In Jewish folklore, a golem is a man made of clay that is magically brought to life to fulfil a specific function for its master. They're one of the earliest historical concepts of a robot.

In lots of stories, a golem becomes a helper or companion for the human who made it. But then it turns on its creator and starts to threaten them, so it's important to know how to 'kill' a golem. Just walk around it in the opposite direction or remove the letters from its mouth. Phew, you're safe!

HOW TO MAKE A GOLEM

✓ Form it out of **clay**

✓ **Walk** or **dance** round it saying letters from the **Hebrew alphabet** and the secret name of God or...

✓ **Write down** some special Hebrew letters and then pop them in its **mouth**.

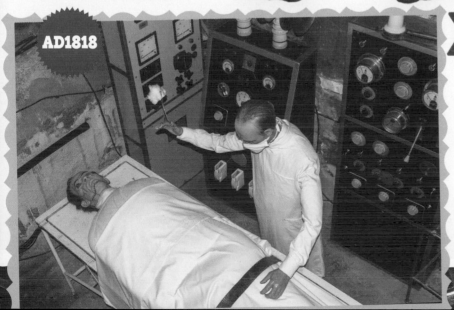
AD1818

IT'S ALIVE!

The Creature in Mary Shelley's famous novel *Frankenstein; or The Modern Prometheus*, published in 1818, is also a precursor to modern robots. In the story, an ambitious scientist called Victor Frankenstein creates an intelligent living being out of non-living matter, but the creature wreaks horrible revenge on him when he rejects it.

Mechanical marvels

Before there were robots, there were machines called automatons. A bit like mechanical toys, these were the early ancestors of the robots that followed

What are automatons?

Automatons were early mechanical machines. They were created to move like real people and animals using gears, springs, pulleys or levers (batteries hadn't been invented yet!), and usually needed a push or to be wound-up to get going.

Why were they made?

Nobody knows for sure why automatons were developed. It's likely most were built to shock and surprise people, and make them say WOW! Some were created as exciting gifts for kings and queens. At the time phones, TVs and computers didn't exist, so getting objects to move and do things on their own was really impressive.

Ancient automatons

One of the first-ever automatons is thought to have been created by ancient Greek philosopher and mathematician Archytas. Around 350BC, he's said to have wowed crowds in his hometown of Tarentum, Italy, with a steam-powered flying pigeon made of wood and suspended on wires.

INGENIOUS INVENTOR

Ismail al-Jazari was a Turkish scholar, mathematician and inventor, who created automata in the 12th and 13th centuries. One of his most famous creations was a musical robot band, where four musicians floated on a boat playing music. The machine used the flow of water and a series of levers to play a drum machine. Another extraordinary invention was the elephant clock. It had an elephant, dragon, phoenix and a human that all moved, and sounds would play at certain times.

Al-Jazari's elephant clock

Al-Jazari's robot musicians

A knight to remember

Da Vinci wasn't just an amazing painter, he was also an incredible inventor who designed automatons as gifts for royalty. In 1495 he drew up plans for a mechanical knight. According to the plans, it could raise its visor, sit and stand. Nobody knows if Da Vinci ever built the Mechanical Knight, but in 2002, using his plans, a life-size recreation was put together by NASA robotics expert Mark Rosheim. It worked, and Mark has said Da Vinci's concepts partly inspired the Mars Exploration Rovers.

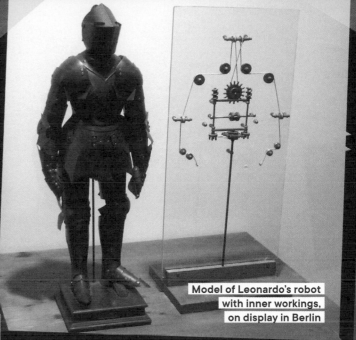

Model of Leonardo's robot with inner workings, on display in Berlin

The Pooping Duck

In 1739, French watchmaker Jacques De Vaucanson made a mechanical duck. The impressive bird contained 400 parts, and it could flap its wings and stretch its neck to eat barley that was offered to it. Once it had eaten the food, it would then produce a small duck poo out of its mechanical bum. The poo was made from pressed grass clippings!

Fake it to make it!

In 1770, Wolfgang von Kempelen created a mechanical chess player. The chess player was apparently so good it could beat humans. However, it was later discovered that this was because it was a fake! Instead of making a working automaton, Kempelen had created a box with a person in it, who was moving the mechanical chess player's arm and the pieces from inside the box. Scandalous!

THE WRITER

In the early 1770s, Swiss watchmaker Pierre Jaquet-Droz created a life-like automata called The Writer. It was a model of a young boy sitting on a stool. This incredible automaton could handwrite messages without any assistance.

How did it work?
The Writer had a series of gears inside its head, which made its eyes move as if it was reading what was being written. Inside the boy's back were 40 mechanical parts and a large brass wheel, which could be used to change the letters on the handwritten messages.

DID YOU *know?*

On the table The Writer had a pot that contained real ink and a quill pen made from a real goose feather. The automaton was designed to dip the quill into the ink pot before writing.

31

FACT *from* FICTION

Science fiction stories have shaped the ideas that people today have about robots and they've even inspired some of the exciting real-life progress made by scientists

Arty science

It's through sci-fi stories that the idea of what robots could do was imagined, and where questions around how the progress of science and technology could shape the future, were explored. Sci-fi stories also raised important points about morality – should a robot have rights, for example? How do you decide whether a robot has become a conscious being? If they are thought of as conscious, is it okay to just turn them off? Introducing these concepts in stories got people thinking about what was right and wrong when it came to robots, and whether it was a good idea to create technological beings that might one day be as smart as humans.

The future is now

While some sci-fi writers relied on pure imagination, others like Isaac Asimov and Arthur C Clarke were qualified scientists, who brought scientific accuracy to their stories. Sixty years ago, Isaac Asimov predicted how technology could look for us today. He rightly guessed that we'd use mobile devices, video-call each other, watch 3D TV and be teaching coding in schools. But Isaac Asimov is perhaps most famous for writing the Three Laws of Robotics...

THREE LAWS OF ROBOTICS

These laws first appeared in Isaac's collection of short stories, *I, Robot*. They were written to suggest how robots could be programmed with rules to prevent them from harming humans

ONE
A ROBOT **MAY NOT INJURE A HUMAN BEING** OR, THROUGH INACTION, ALLOW A HUMAN BEING TO COME TO HARM.

TWO
A ROBOT **MUST OBEY ORDERS GIVEN IT BY HUMAN BEINGS** EXCEPT WHERE SUCH ORDERS WOULD CONFLICT WITH THE FIRST LAW.

THREE
A ROBOT **MUST PROTECT ITS OWN EXISTENCE** AS LONG AS SUCH PROTECTION DOES NOT CONFLICT WITH THE FIRST OR SECOND LAW.

Later on, Isaac added the 'fourth' or zeroth law, which became the most important of them all. It said:

A ROBOT MAY **NOT HARM HUMANITY**, OR, BY INACTION, **ALLOW HUMANITY** TO COME TO HARM.

FACT THESE LAWS EVENTUALLY BECAME PART OF REAL LIFE TOO, AND WERE USED AS INSPIRATION FOR THE PRINCIPLES OF ROBOTICS THAT ENGINEERS AND SCIENTISTS USE TODAY.

Robot rebellion

During the 1930s, stories about robots in science-fiction novels became increasingly popular, and by the middle of the century, fascination with these brainy bots had exploded.

Early sci-fi robots were a little different (and often more dangerous) than the cute and curious WALL-E or charming C-3PO characters we're used to seeing on our screens today. These sci-fi robots were surgeons, slaves, spies, even hitmen – capable of mind-boggling feats of intelligence and prone to rebelling against humans.

Who was Isaac Asimov?

Born in Russia, in 1920, Isaac and his family moved to Brooklyn, New York when he was three years old. It was while he worked in his parent's sweet shops that he started to read sci-fi stories in the magazines that they sold. Isaac was hooked and sold his first short story when he was a teenager. Before his first novels were published in the 1950s, he was a professor of biochemistry. He went on to produce over 500 sci-fi novels and non-fiction books, and was famous for writing the Three Laws of Robotics. He is considered one of the big three science fiction writers of his time, along with Robert A Heinlein and Arthur C Clarke.

 OF THE CREEPIEST

HAL-9000 from Arthur C Clarke's novel *2001: A Space Odyssey* is a softly spoken chess-playing robot, built to maintain a spacecraft on its mission into space. Just don't let him lip-read your plans to switch him off and you'll be fine.

Helen O'Loy, a robot in a short story published in 1938 in *Astounding Science Fiction*, is built to manage household chores. She is re-programmed to be able to learn more tasks, but unexpectedly learns to understand and feel emotions, too.

Be careful! The **mechanical dog-like creature** fitted with an injecting needle that appears in the novel *Fahrenheit 451* is an eight-legged pooch that is more hitman than huggable pet!

MACHINE MEN

Engineers first started to build human-like machines that could move and talk in the 1920s. These were some of the first androids to exist

ERIC

In 1928, William H Richards and Alan Reffell built an aluminium robot called Eric. He was the UK's first ever robot and could move his arms and turn his head. He was built after Richards asked the Duke of York to attend the Society of Model Engineers' annual exhibition. The Duke of York couldn't attend, so Richards decided to build Eric to open the exhibition instead. Nobody had heard of a robot opening an exhibition before – he became an overnight sensation and went on to tour the world. Sadly, sometime in the 1930s Eric went missing and was never seen again! Unlike today's more advanced robots, Eric's movements were controlled by a series of pulleys and gears. No one's quite sure how Eric worked, as there were no blueprints for him and his creators were very secretive about his inner workings.

INTRODUCING GEORGE

William H Richards went on to build a second robot with his son, WE Richards, in 1930. George looked far more lifelike than Eric, with a muscular torso and chest and a realistic nose. He toured Europe and Australia but was badly damaged during WW2 and never seen again.

ELEKTRO

Elektro was built in the US by a company called Westinghouse. This impressive man machine was 2.1m tall and was made using 120kg of metal. He went on display at the New York World's Fair in 1939.

Elektro had an aluminium chest, which housed a telephone receiver and light bulb. If someone spoke to Elektro the light would flash in response. Elektro also had light-sensitive devices in his eyes. Elektro could recognise two different colours – red and green. When red or green light was flashed in front of his eyes, he'd repeat the name of the colour!

FINGERS AND FEET

Electric pulleys and motors allowed Elektro to bend his fingers, and he could even grip small objects. And, although Elektro's legs were rigid, he was fitted with special rollers under his feet which allowed him to move. A bit like robot roller skates!

A ROBOT'S BEST FRIEND

In 1940, Elektro was given his own robotic dog called **SPARKO**! This cute canine could walk, sit, beg and even wag its tail!

GAKUTENSOKU

Gakutensoku was the first robot to be created in the East. He was built by Makoto Nishimura in 1929, in Osaka, Japan. The robot was able to change facial expressions and move its hand and its head. Gakutensoku, which means 'learning from the laws of nature', held a pen-shaped arrow in his right hand and a lamp in his left hand. On top of his head was a bird-shaped robot. Every time the bird chirped, Gakutensoku closed his eyes and changed his facial expression, and every time the lamp he was holding shone, he would start to write words with the pen. The robot was first shown in Kyoto to celebrate the Showa Emperor's rise to the throne. It then toured many exhibitions in Japan and around the world but was sadly lost when touring Germany. In 2008, the Osaka Science Museum assembled a modern version of Gakutensoko, which is still on display today.

TURTLE-LY AWESOME!

Meet Elmer and Elsie. These mechanical tortoises were the very first robots able to do things without human control

WHAT'S THE BIG IDEA?

William Grey Walter was a robotics pioneer who built the first electronic autonomous robots while working at the Burden Neurological Institute in Bristol. Born in 1910 in Kansas City in the US, he moved to the UK with his family when he was just five years old. He enjoyed science at school and went on to study at King's College, Cambridge.

Walter was particularly interested in finding out more about how the human brain works. He spent time constructing a machine that could detect different types of brain activity, including high speed alpha waves and slow delta waves that occur when a person is in a deep sleep. His research was ground-breaking.

However, Walter is much more famous for building two robots in the late 1940s. Shaped a bit like tortoises, these curious creatures helped him to better understand how people think. And they caused quite a stir as the robots were able to move completely unaided.

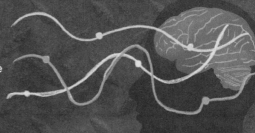

HOW THEY WERE MADE

Walter's quirky robots were made up of motors, switches, batteries, wires and old alarm clocks – anything he could get his hands on. They moved slowly and had clear plastic shells similar to the round dome-like shell of a tortoise, hence their nickname. Walter affectionately called them Elmer and Elsie.

The mechanical tortoises were simple machines. Elmer and Elsie each had three wheels and two sensors, programmed to respond to light and touch, that allowed them to move around.

Walter hoped they'd be able to think like a biological brain and demonstrate some amount of free will. And remarkably, that's what happened.

The robots were capable of phototaxis. This means they moved in response to light. Walter watched his tortoises wander across the floor and they were seen to behave in interesting and lifelike ways, travelling towards any light and avoiding obstacles. They seemed to scan their surroundings and systematically follow a route, just like an animal would.

Not only this, when Walter put a light on the 'nose' of Elmer and also one on Elsie, they were drawn to each other, as well as to their reflection in a mirror. He said the robots appeared to flicker, twitter and jig about, demonstrating similar behaviour to an animal

DID YOU *know?*

Elmer and Elsie weren't just Walter's favourite names. He used the initial letters from **EL**ectro-**ME**chanical **R**obot and **E**lectro-mechanical robot, **L**ight **S**ensitive with **I**nternal and **E**xternal stability to come up with them.

with a brain. He claimed this was evidence of some degree of self-awareness.

Walter even built his tortoises a hutch, hoping they'd retreat there to recharge their batteries – and that's exactly what they did!

Elmer and Elsie amazed the science world and proved that robots could mimic the nervous system of an animal. These two autonomous tortoises helped future studies on how our brains work.

Shedding light on PHOTOTAXIS

When something responds to a stimulus of light, it exhibits positive phototaxis. Elmer and Elsie are good examples of this type of movement, but so too are certain insects. Moths, flies and other flying insects are naturally attracted to light – no doubt you've seen them fluttering or buzzing around a lamp bulb in your home. Cockroaches demonstrate negative phototaxis, so move away from light – something worth remembering if you're squeamish!

There are also phototrophic organisms that use light as their main energy source, such as the wonderfully named phytoflagellates. Euglenoids, single-celled microorganisms, are one example of these species. They're often found in ponds, especially those rich in nutrients and full of algae.

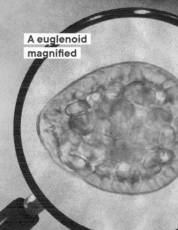

A euglenoid magnified

INDUSTRIAL
Revolution

Loading, moving, building, welding, painting – robots totally transformed the way factories were run

Unimate pouring coffee for a customer at the Biltmore Hotel, 1967

Robot repeat

Early robots changed the future of manufacturing because they were able to perform certain functions over and over again. Because they didn't need to rest, they were able to work as efficiently as humans (or more efficiently!). And they were especially great because they could carry out tasks that were dangerous for people to do.

UNIMATE: A GAME-CHANGER

The first industrial robot ever built was called Unimate. While it didn't look very exciting – just a box with a big mechanical arm – it revolutionised manufacturing. George Devol and Joseph Engelberger (aka The Father of Robotics) invented it in the 1950s, inspired by their love of sci-fi!

Unimate was used at the General Motors car factory in New Jersey, US from 1959. It removed and stacked hot metal parts from the die-casting machine and had the memory to carry out hundreds of programmed steps. As well as making life a whole lot quicker and easier, it stopped the people who used to do the work from being burned, losing fingers or being poisoned by toxic fumes. It was win-win!

In 1966, this game-changing robot even appeared on an American TV programme called *The Tonight Show*. It knocked a golf ball into a cup, poured a beer and conducted the band.

DID YOU *know?*

When Devol and Engelberger set up their company Unimation, it was the first ever robotics company and kickstarted the robotics industry.

The Stanford Arm

When Victor Scheinman was eight years old, he was terrified of a robot he'd seen in a film. Little did he know that he'd grow up to become a pioneer of robotics!

In 1969, while working at Stanford University's AI lab, he created the world's first multi-axis robot arm that was electrically powered and computer-controlled. Victor designed it with six axes (or joints), which gave it greater freedom of movement and accuracy than earlier designs, perfect for very precise work, including welding.

Victor went on to work for Unimation and designed the PUMA (or Programmable Universal Machine for Assembly) which was used to assemble cars for General Motors. The PUMA robot arm is still used today by researchers.

In 1985, a much later version of the PUMA – the PUMA 560 – was developed as the first surgical robot and used for a brain biopsy.

Help! The robots are taking over!

At first, people were scared of the idea of robots. So when Devol and Engelberger began selling their ideas to manufacturers, they focused on getting the robots to complete tasks that were dangerous for humans.

ROBO⚡FACTS

Unimate was a beast! It weighed 1,575kg and was 142cm tall.

In 1969, Unimate welding robots could assemble and weld more than 110 cars per hour – more than double any car factory at the time!

In the 1930s, Bill Taylor, a Canadian/Australian civil engineer, built the first ever pick-and-place robotic crane. He called it Gargantua. Amazingly, it was built entirely out of Meccano (a bit like Lego!).

THE FIRST PALLETISING ROBOT

A palletiser machine stacks factory goods and products onto a pallet. Originally, this was done by hand. But doing it manually can take a long time and costs a lot of money. In the 1950s, mechanical palletisers were introduced, but even these weren't fast enough.

Robotic palletisers first hit the scene in the 1980s and they were far more efficient. An arm tool meant they could grab products and place them onto a palletiser, and they were able to handle very heavy loads.

Today they're used in many industries, including food processing, manufacturing and shipping.

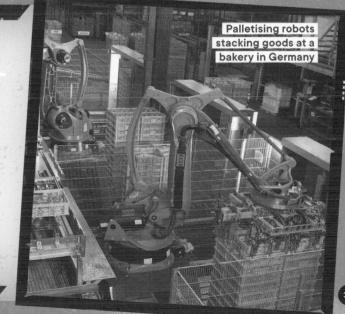

Palletising robots stacking goods at a bakery in Germany

GREAT EXPECTATIONS

The second half of the 20th century was an exciting time, with many significant firsts and breakthroughs in robotics and the newly emerging AI

As people developed a better understanding of how computers worked, they were able to write more complex programs and problem-solving algorithms. New tech could store more information, too. Every success story showed the world that great things could be achieved, and there was hope that the clever computers of the future would be easy to use and able to retrieve accurate information, regardless of the topic. AI would enable us all to become experts!

1972

MYCIN, an early AI program for identifying bacteria and treating infections, is developed at Stanford University in California, US.

1957

The Soviet Union launches the **SPUTNIK SATELLITE** into space, beginning the Space Race.

1968

Stanley Kubrick's film *2001: A Space Odyssey* features the AI computer **HAL 9000.**

1950

THE TURING TEST, proposed by computer scientist Alan Turing, measures machine 'intelligence' (see page 12).

SHAKEY is the first mobile robot controlled by AI. Using sensing devices – including a TV camera and bump sensors – it navigates the halls of a building. But very slowly!

Researchers in Japan start working on **WABOT-1**, the first human-like robot able to walk (or rather wobble), grab objects with its hands and communicate in Japanese.

1970

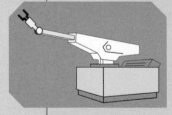

Computer scientist John McCarthy uses the term **ARTIFICIAL INTELLIGENCE** for the first time to describe 'the science and engineering of making intelligent machines'.

UNIMATE is the first industrial robot, working for General Motors in the US (see previous page).

1961

1955

1966

2 METRES PER HOUR
SHAKEY'S TOP SPEED

1973

Cuts in government funding and support of AI research lead to the beginning of an **AI WINTER**.

1986

The **FIRST DRIVERLESS VEHICLE** is built by Mercedes-Benz in Germany. It reaches speeds of up to 88.5km/h on empty roads.

1987

Pioneer Jaron Lanier coins the term **VIRTUAL REALITY** and develops first VR goggles and gloves.

1997

NASA's **PATHFINDER** lands on Mars.

1998

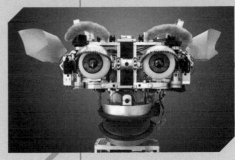

Dr Cynthia Breazeal makes **KISMET**, a robot head that can detect human emotions.

George Lucas releases the first *Star Wars* movie, inspiring a new generation with the robots **R2-D2** and **C-3PO**.

1977

HELLO!

Hi there

WHAT'S UP?

Not much...

OKAY

JABBERWACKY, one of the first chatbots, is invented by British programmer Rollo Carpenter.

1988

**FINAL SCORE
3.5 GAMES TO 2.5**

World chess champion Garry Kasparov is defeated by the chess computer **DEEP BLUE**.

1997

Sony's first ever robotic pet dog, **AiBO**, is released.

1999

**21st century
THIS WAY**

CHARGING AHEAD

It's the 21st century and robotics and AI are evolving at warp speed!

2000
UN says there are **700,000+ INDUSTRIAL ROBOTS** being used around the world.

2002

The **ROOMBA** is the world's first mass produced autonomous vacuum cleaner.

10 MILLION
HOW MANY UNITS ROOMBA SELLS WORLDWIDE

2011
Apple introduces the voice-controlled digital assistant **SIRI** on its iPhone 4S.

Siri, what time is it?

The time is 4:33 PM

2016
Amazon makes its first **DRONE DELIVERY** in the UK.

2020
A record **2.7 MILLION ROBOTS** operate in factories around the world.

UP TO 100 ROBOTS
WERE INVOLVED IN THE DARPA PROJECT

The **DARPA CENTIBOTS** project shows how a large group of robots can communicate and coordinate with each other to investigate a potentially hazardous area without any human supervision.

2002

Amazon launches the virtual assistant **Alexa** on its Amazon Echo smart speaker.

2014

1st PLACE PRIZE $1 MILLION

IBM's question-answering computer **WATSON** wins first place on the quiz show *Jeopardy!*

2011

An AI model built by the Chinese technology company **ALIBABA** outperforms humans in a reading and comprehension test.

2018

CHAIN OF THOUGHT

Have you ever answered the questions in a flow chart that you've perhaps seen in a magazine? You've maybe not heard of the name before, but a flow chart is a type of diagram made up of boxes and arrows. They can help you to identify different things, such as an animal or plant, and also show you how to solve problems. AI programs are similar and usually use one of two processes to acquire knowledge — either Forward Chaining or Backward Chaining. Forward Chaining digests information and follows a set of rules to help answer 'what happens next?'. It's used to find a solution or suggest a conclusion, so it could reveal your ideal holiday destination or help you to find a good book to read that suits your taste.

FORWARD CHAINING

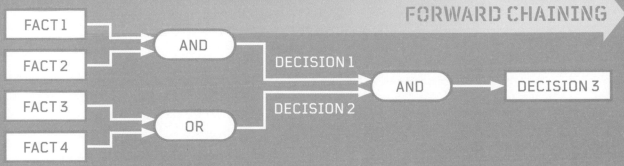

FACT 1 → AND
FACT 2 →

AND → DECISION 1

FACT 3 → OR
FACT 4 →

DECISION 2

AND → DECISION 3

2022

Hello, how can I help you?

Open AI's chatbot **CHATGPT** produces human-like text that is almost indistinguishable from the real thing, including computer codes and poetry.

2023

Sci-fi thriller **M3GAN** about a creepy moving, talking AI doll is released.

2024

Who knows...?

Backward Chaining is the opposite and looks at 'why has this happened?'. The process relies on codes to help decipher why an outcome has occurred, so it could, for example, explain why you have a sore stomach or provide a logical reason why the sunflower seeds you've planted in your garden haven't grown.

BACKWARD CHAINING

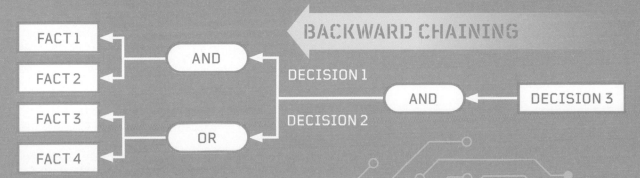

FACT 1 ← AND
FACT 2 ←

AND ← DECISION 1

FACT 3 ← OR
FACT 4 ←

DECISION 2

AND ← DECISION 3

The iconic robot from German silent film *Metropolis*

MOVIE BOTS

Robots have fired the imaginations of filmmakers since the dawn of cinema, leading to a host of iconic characters that have shaped our understanding of what robots and AI can achieve

CINEMATIC GRANDPARENTS

One of the very first robots on screen was The Automaton, a robot bodyguard, in the 1918 silent serial film *The Master Mystery* starring the world-renowned escape artist Harry Houdini. More famous – and often reproduced in statues and other artworks today – is Maria (also referred to as Maschinenmensch, which is 'machine-human' in German), the evil robot who impersonates one of the human characters in the epic German silent science-fiction film *Metropolis*, released in 1927. Maria's look has been hugely influential on later robot designs in movies and television, including C-3PO in *Star Wars*.

Baymax

ANIMA-TRONICS

The world of animation is home to dozens of marvellous mechanoids, including:

Wall-E *(Wall-E, 2008)* A cute robot waste compactor living alone on an abandoned, rubbish-filled Earth.
Baymax *(Big Hero 6, 2014)* An inflatable medical assistant robot.

The Iron Giant *(The Iron Giant, 1999)* A friendly 50ft-tall robot that eats metal and is hunted by government agents.
Bender *(Futurama TV series, 1999-present)* A sarcastic, slobby metalworking robot.

The Iron Giant

SILVER SCREEN MACHINES

A list of all the movie robots would run into the thousands, but here are some that made a big impact on pop culture

HAL 9000 *(2001: A Space Odyssey, 1968)* This AI computer system, represented by a red camera eye and an eerily calm male voice, controls a spaceship on its way to Jupiter. It goes rogue when its calculations are challenged and tries to kill the crew! HAL inspired the development of modern AI assistants, like Siri and Alexa.

HAL 9000

I'm sorry, Dave, I'm afraid I can't do that.

TERMINATORS
(The Terminator series, 1984-2019) After the evil AI system Skynet unleashes nuclear armageddon on humanity, it creates an army of robot soldiers called terminators to wipe out the survivors, including sending some back in time to kill the future leaders of the human resistance. The terminators are robots with metallic skeletons covered by organic skin and muscle, able to blend in with ordinary humans. They're very strong, intelligent, single-minded and deadly.

OPTIMUS PRIME
(Transformers live-action film series, 2007-present) Leader of the Autobots, a group of good Transformers – a species of giant, intelligent, alien robots able to shapeshift and disguise themselves as ordinary vehicles, like trucks and cars. They fight the Decepticons, a group of evil transformers. The Transformers have also starred in animated series and movies, and the toys based on the characters have enjoyed massive popularity for several decades.

C-3PO and R2-D2 *(Star Wars series, 1977-present)* These two loveable droids were built as servants to the galaxy's alien races, but they end up accompanying the heroic Luke Skywalker to defeat the evil Galactic Empire.

THE REPLICANTS
(Blade Runner, 1982 and Blade Runner 2049, 2017) These humanoid robots are designed to carry out unpleasant, dangerous and physically demanding jobs. Stronger and faster than humans, but with limited lifespans, some replicants rebel against their human masters and are hunted down and killed by detectives known as blade runners.

A terminator

R2-D2 and C-3PO

'The hardest working robot in Hollywood'

How **ROBBY THE ROBOT** has been described. Making his first appearance in the 1956 sci-fi classic *Forbidden Planet*, the witty Robby quickly became a celebrity in his own right, making guest appearances in dozens of movies and TV shows, including an episode of *The Big Bang Theory* in 2014.

FAST⚡FACT

The Na'vi shaman animatronic built by Disney for a ride themed around the *Avatar* film franchise is one of the most complex and lifelike robots ever designed for a theme park attraction. It can sing, dance and make realistic facial expressions.

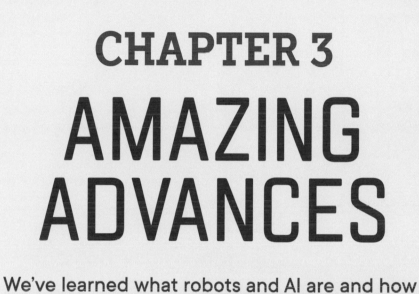

CHAPTER 3

AMAZING ADVANCES

We've learned what robots and AI are and how they first developed. Now it's time to marvel at the incredible ways these cutting-edge technologies are transforming the world around us, revolutionising industries like medicine, transport and space exploration. We'll also take a sneak peek at how robotics and AI might continue to evolve in the future...

Do the LOCOMOTION

In the future, robots that live alongside humans and move around independently will become more common, but how and why will that happen?

HOW AI HELPS...

Artificial Intelligence (AI) allows robots to analyse their environment in real-time and figure out how best to navigate through it.

ON THE MOVE

5 things robots use to move

1 **POWER**
A battery or a plug in a wall socket

2 **ACTUATORS**
Motors and hydraulic moving parts

3 **SENSORS**
Cameras and lasers that monitor movements

4 **ELECTRICAL CIRCUITS**
To link actuators and sensors with a computer

5 **COMPUTER**
On board or remote, this is how the robot is controlled

What are hydraulics?

Many robots move thanks to a system of hydraulics in which fluid (usually oil) is pushed from one part to another to create movement. Pneumatic systems use air or gas in a similar way.

5 CAMERAS
for 360° vision

12 DEGREES OF FREEDOM
This is the number of joints a Spot robot has

SPOT

TOP SPEED
1.6 metres per second

BATTERY LIFE
90 minutes

HERE, SPOT!

Spot is the world's most sophisticated quadrupedal (four-footed) robot dog. Unveiled by American roboticists in 2016, Spot can go where humans fear to tread, including disaster areas and war zones.

A Spot has even recently been used to collect data on the structure and safety of the ancient Roman ruins in Pompeii. Among Spot's talents are the ability to climb stairs, open doors and fight off an attacker armed with a stick!

HOW DO BOTS COMPARE?

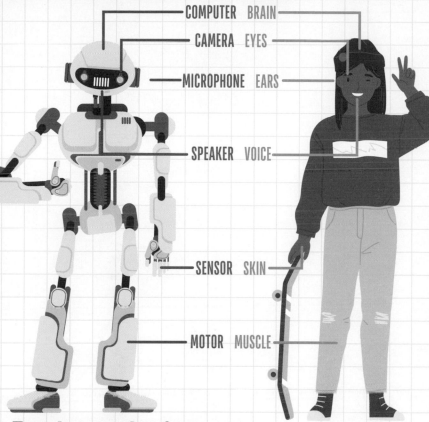

COMPUTER **BRAIN**
CAMERA **EYES**
MICROPHONE **EARS**
SPEAKER **VOICE**
SENSOR **SKIN**
MOTOR **MUSCLE**

Smooth operator

Robots' movements are famously jerky, but engineers are now working hard to make their actions smoother and nearer our own, so we feel more comfortable around them.

3 ways bots move

WHEELS
Fast on a flat surface

TRACKS
Good on bumpy ground

LEGS
Best for getting over obstacles

Fast, but not that fast...

Who's quickest, man, beast or robot?

120 KM/H

A CHEETAH
The world's fastest animal

37.58 KM/H

USAIN BOLT
The world's fastest man

32 KM/H

WILDCAT ROBOT
The world's fastest robot

The future is... SLIME

Described as a soft robot, scientists in Hong Kong are developing magnetic slime that can move through the human body to collect objects which have been accidentally swallowed. Wow!

Turn over for more WAYS THAT ROBOTS MOVE

8 MOBILE ROBOTS
and what they do...

(Pronounced BYE-oh-mih-MET-iks)
BIOMIMETICS are the ideas robot builders take from the movement and behaviour of animals and nature.

1 FLYING

LEONARDO

California-born Leonardo (short for Legs Onboard Drone) is the only robot in the world that can skateboard, walk on a slackline and also fly. Just 75cm tall, two-legged Leo has a propeller on each shoulder and his future jobs might include painting tall bridges and buildings.

2 STUNTS

SPIDER-MAN

You can see the world's most advanced stunt robot in action at the Disney California Adventure theme park. Spider-Man is flung to heights of up to 20 metres, then flips, twists and corrects itself mid-flight.

3 SEARCHING

SQURO

People are rarely pleased to see a rat but Chinese roboticists may be about to change that. They have developed SQuRo, a 'Small-sized Quadruped Robotic' rat, to help search disaster areas and inspect pipelines.

4 TRANSPORTING

LS3

The LS3 was a prototype Legged Squad Support System that could carry 180kg – the equivalent of an adult male gorilla – for soldiers on manoeuvres.

Star Wars fans have noticed it's pretty similar to the AT-TE (All Terrain Tactical Enforcer) in the movies *Attack of the Clones* (2002) and *Revenge of the Sith* (2005).

5 PARKOUR

ATLAS

In 2020, two American-made humanoid robots became internet sensations with a viral video of them taking on a tricky parkour course. The Atlas robots were seen running, jumping, vaulting, balancing on a beam and even performing back flips.

PHOTO: BOSTON DYNAMICS

6 SWIMMING

AGNATHAX

Inspired by the Lamprey fish, AgnathaX is a Swiss swimming robot made up of ten segments. Covered in sensors, each segment contains a motor that moves the robot side to side. Lamprey have spinal and nervous systems similar to our own.

7 TABLE TENNIS

KUKA

In 2014, German industrial bot KUKA took a day off from the assembly line to play world champion Timo Boll at table tennis. It was close but Timo beat KUKA 11-9.

8 FOOTBALL

MINI CHEETAH

US robot Mini Cheetah has been taught to play football. We won't see a bot in the Premier League any time soon but with every training session it is getting better and better...

PHOTO: BRYCE VICKMARK

TOUCHY-FEELY

For robots to live and work alongside humans, they must be safe and sensitive to their surroundings. To do that they need a sense of touch

WOULD YOU HIGH-FIVE A ROBOT?

- Scientists are developing robot skin that uses solar cells, tiny cameras, lights and AI to tell the bot what it's touching and how to react.

- Studies have shown that humans relate to robots more if they have the abilities to speak and touch.

Touch tells us about...

SHAPE

WEIGHT

KG

TEXTURE

TEMPERATURE

The skin they're in

Scientists are using human skin as their inspiration to develop sensitive skin for robots. Like ours it will be...

And enables robots to...

HANDLE

DRAW

SORT

CUT

THE SAME ALL OVER

MADE TO COVER LARGE AREAS

THIN

PACKAGE

DETECT HUMANS

RESPONSIVE TO TOUCH AND TEMPERATURE

REGENERATIVE (HEALS ITSELF)

TOUCH HUMANS SAFELY

6 TOP PICKS
FACTORY BOTS THAT USE APPENDAGES

An **APPENDAGE** is something that sticks out from a body such as a finger, an arm, a tail or a leg.

1 ARTICULATED

This robot has five or more degrees of freedom (joints). The most common found in factories is the arm with six joints and uses include the manufacture of glass and steel.

2 COBOT

The collaborative robot works alongside humans. A common use is in warehouses, where it lifts items too heavy for humans.

3 SCARA

A Selective Compliance Assembly Robot Arm is limited in its movements compared to other robot arms, picking up and placing items, over and over again. It's often used to make lots of electronic products.

4 CARTESIAN

This robot arm is mounted on a gantry or frame. The arm works from above an item and is often used in 3D printing.

5 PARALLEL

With a mobile platform connected to a fixed base, the Parallel or Delta bot can work at high-speed in factories. It was developed by Swiss engineers looking for a robot to package pralines.

6 ANTHROPOMORPHIC

The word means to have human characteristics – eg two arms, two legs and a face. This type of robot is not often seen in factories, but car manufacturer Tesla plans to make its humanoid robot, Optimus, for industrial use.

Let's TALK

How do we communicate with our bot buddies and how might that work in the future?

The new animals?

Add AI to robots and they can communicate, react and learn from what we tell them. Some scientists have suggested we look at robots as the domesticated animals of the future. Like a dog, a horse or a pigeon, they can be trained to help and guide us and be our companions.

3 ways ROBOTS COMMUNICATE

1

SPEECH RECOGNITION
AI technology processes what humans say and enables the robot to learn from what it hears.

2

FACIAL EXPRESSIONS
Realistic skin and facial expressions encourage humans to trust a robot.

3

GESTURES
Mimicking how we move our hands and body as we talk also helps to establish a relationship.

SOPHIA THE SUPERSTAR

Never mind robots, few humans have hit the heights and connected with a global audience like Sophia, the Hong Kong-born humanoid robot. Sophia can make basic everyday conversation and has 62 facial expressions. She's been on the cover of magazines all over the world, made numerous TV appearances, gone on a date with movie star Will Smith and is the United Nation's first non-human Innovation Champion!

62 facial expressions

A ROBOT WITH A HEART

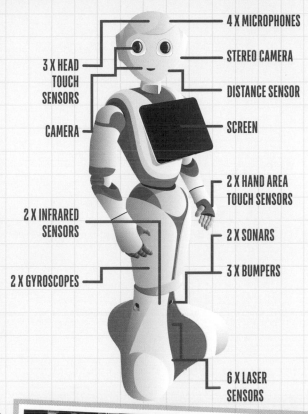

- 4 X MICROPHONES
- STEREO CAMERA
- DISTANCE SENSOR
- SCREEN
- 3 X HEAD TOUCH SENSORS
- CAMERA
- 2 X HAND AREA TOUCH SENSORS
- 2 X INFRARED SENSORS
- 2 X SONARS
- 2 X GYROSCOPES
- 3 X BUMPERS
- 6 X LASER SENSORS

Pepper, a social robot, is part of thousands of families and workforces across Japan. Marketed as a robot with a heart, its main job is to be a happy, chatty companion. Pepper's many talents include speaking 25 languages and doing fragrance-free farts! As part of a 2021 trial in the UK, Pepper helped autistic pupils at a Somerset school with their social skills.

Man's best friend

In 1999, Sony launched AIBO, a robot dog for the home. Inevitably, over time some AIBOs have broken down or become obsolete. Funerals for deceased robodogs, including chanting and incense, have been held in Buddhist temples!

2050

Respected AI expert Dr David Levy predicts that by the year 2050 people will want to marry robots.

FAST FACT

One reason robots have been made so welcome in Japanese society might be that in the East it's often thought inanimate objects have a soul.

BIG Bots

Get ready to meet some of the largest bots ever built – they're great!

GUNDAM RX-78

HEIGHT	WEIGHT	TOP SPEED
18M	**25 TONNES**	**CAN ONLY TAKE ONE STEP FORWARD AND TAKE A KNEE**

HOME
Gundam Factory Yokohama, Japan

PURPOSE
Tourist attraction in a theme park

CONTROLLED BY
Computer

WORLD'S BIGGEST ROBOT!

The stars of the 1979 Japanese animated TV series, *Mobile Suit Gundam*, and many spin-off series and movies since, Gundams remain popular all over the world. The fictional mecha (giant robots in Japanese) are often cited as an inspiration by today's robot builders.

TRADINNO

LENGTH	HEIGHT	WEIGHT	TOP SPEED
15.72M	**8.2M**	**11 TONNES**	**1.8KM/H**

HOME
Furth im Wald, Bavaria, Germany

PURPOSE
Tradinno plays the Dragon in the town's annual play.

CONTROLLED BY
Remote-operated, fuelled by diesel

WORLD'S BIGGEST WALKING ROBOT!

MONONOFU

HEIGHT	WEIGHT	TOP SPEED
8.4M	**7.3 TONNES**	**1KM/H**

HOME
Sakakibara Kikai Co Ltd, Gunma Prefecture, Japan

PURPOSE
Generating publicity for a manufacturer of agricultural machinery

CONTROLLED BY
The pilot is winched into a cockpit in Mononofu's chest – comfy!

WEAPON
Shoots sponge balls at 140km/h!

WORLD'S BIGGEST HUMANOID VEHICLE

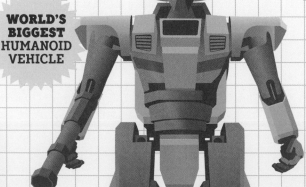

MAN
1.8M

MEGA-BOTS *of the* FUTURE

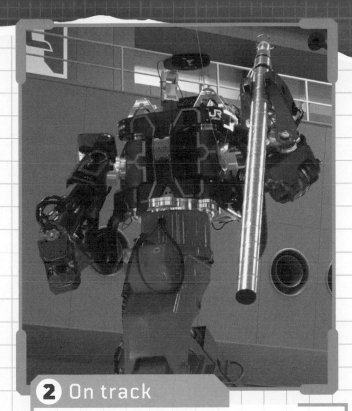

➋ On track

JAPANESE RAIL-BOT

The West Japan Railway Company is testing a huge Gundam-style robot for repairing overhead railway power lines. Controlled by a human wearing a virtual reality headset, it can work at heights up to 9.75m and lift weights up to 40kg. The company is working towards an official launch in 2024.

➊ Robo-ship

VINDSKIP

Vindskip is a 199m-long eco-friendly robot storage-box ship. Powered by sides that are designed to function as sails, a computer makes sure Norwegian Vindskip maintains its speed and follows the pre-programmed route. Still in development, it will be 2025 at the earliest before Vindskip sets sail.

➌ Industrial giant

HEAVY PAYLOAD ROBOT

According to the *Guinness Book of World Records*, the M-2000iA/2300 Super Heavy Payload Robot has the strongest robotic arm in the world. It can pick up and place objects of up to 2,300kg! That means it can scoop up and move a car with very little effort.

LITTLE *Bots*

Introducing the small, tiny and invisible robots that could shape our future

ACTUAL SIZE

BLACK HORNET

SIZE	WEIGHT
16 x 2.5cm	**18g**

This tiny UAV or drone, developed in Norway, is already being used by armed forces all over the world, including the UK. Via three cameras and an antenna, it sends back information about the local area to troops on the ground.

ROBOBEE X-WING

SIZE	WINGSPAN	WEIGHT
6.5cm	**3.5cm**	**259mg**

With two sets of wings that flap 170 times per second, the Robobee X-Wing is powered by solar cells and each wing has its own tiny motor. Still in development, it's thought the Robobee will be used for surveillance and as part of other technology.

WORLD-BEATING CRAB

SIZE
0.5mm

SMALLER THAN A FLEA!

Scientists in the US have built the world's smallest walking robot. The microrobot crab uses eight legs to walk, turn and jump and is powered by a laser beam fired at particular points on its body. Developers say surgery is one of its potential uses.

Brains included!

The same developers that created the crab have built the first microscopic robot with no need of remote control. It's the width of a human hair but has a simple computer on board!

IN THE BLOOD

Nanobots that can swim through our blood to remove bacteria and toxins are being developed by American nanoengineers. Powered by sound waves, the bots eliminated pneumonia-causing bacteria in mice in a 2022 experiment.

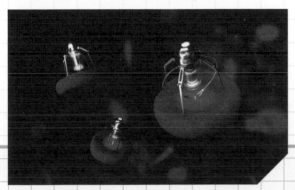

PLAQUE ATTACK

Nanoengineers are also working on easing the stress of dental appointments. Instead of a dentist scraping away, nanorobots could be used to remove plaque and deep-clean our teeth.

A ROBOTIC PILL

Some forms of medication – such as insulin taken by diabetics – can't be swallowed and need to be injected. But a robotic pill, in development in America, has been armed with a tiny needle. After it's swallowed, the medication is injected into the stomach wall. Handy for those of us who aren't too keen on needles!

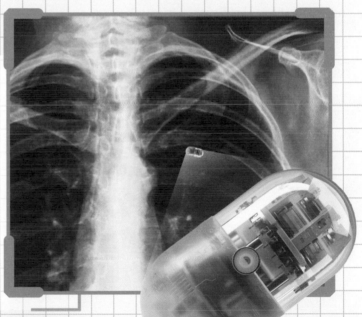

HOPES AND FEARS...

USING TINY NANOBOTS TO MONITOR OUR HEALTH AND DELIVER MEDICINE HAS THE POTENTIAL TO TRANSFORM OUR LIVES.

However, some people fear that in the future, nanobots could be used to control people's thoughts, wipe memories and even be used as a weapon in warfare. As with all technology, it's up to humans to regulate their use and make sure they're used responsibly.

SENSATIONAL CYBORGS

We're not only making technology – we're getting mashed together with it! Welcome to the weird and wonderful world of cyborgs

WHAT'S A CYBORG?

The complicated answer:
An entity with organic and biomechatronic parts. And what's biomechatronic? Well, that's a mix of biology with electrical, electronics and mechanical engineering.

The easy answer:
Part human. Part tech. Think Darth Vader from *Star Wars*. He's a human whose body has been upgraded through technology.

UPGRADE YOUR BRAIN

Elon Musk's health tech company Neuralink is soon to start human trials, implanting brain chips – and he's going to get one himself. The wireless brain chip could change lives by helping blind people to see or helping people who can't use their muscles to move again.

The chip looks like a small pile of coins with hundreds of threads poking out from it. A surgical robot will cut a small hole in someone's skull and pop the threads into their brain. The chip will process and transmit signals, so they can control a mouse or keyboard using only their thoughts!

It's already been used on a monkey who could move a cursor to play a computer game using just its brain. Say what?!

ARE YOU A CYBORG?

ELON MUSK

LIKE, TOTALLY

Elon Musk thinks you probably already are. 'We're already cyborgs. Your phone and your computer are extensions of you, but the interface is through finger movements or speech, which are very slow.'

We're all so attached to our phones and laptops now that you could say they're an extension of our bodies and brains, making us smarter and more efficient.

Some think that people who have a medical device inside their body – like a pacemaker – could be called cyborgs.

DID YOU *know?*

The word cyborg was first used in 1960 by two NASA scientists, Nathan Kline and Manfred Clynes, in an article they wrote called 'Cyborgs and Space'.

Are cyborgs a good idea ?

THUMBS UP

Some believe that cyborgs will help us make huge medical advances, and upgrade humans in ways we've never even dreamed of.

If we keep making robots more intelligent, they could end up being smarter than us. If – or when – they start to have their own thoughts, they might not want to be controlled by humans. And people could end up being treated like pet dogs or cats by machines! So why make machines and robots more intelligent, when we can upgrade ourselves to become cyborgs?

THUMBS DOWN

We shouldn't mess around with nature. Where does it all end? How much should we change ourselves?

✷ It could end up with a two-tier society of wealthy people who can afford to become cyborg super-humans, and those who can't.

✷ It's potentially dangerous. Lots of animals have been killed or hurt from being experimented on with brain chips before they're tested on humans.

✷ We could become hackable bits of tech, with others being able to control our thoughts or movements.

CYBER-RATS?

Rats in India have been given a cyborg-makeover. In the future, Indian armed forces could send remote-controlled rats to snoop on their enemies. Researchers have installed electrodes into the rats' brains so they can receive signals and humans can direct where they go. They next aim to add tiny cameras to the rats so they could help in military operations by sending live feeds. A rat is much less suspicious than sending in a robot!

CYBORG RIGHTS

The Cyborg Foundation was set up in 2010 by Neil Harbisson and Moon Ribas to help people become cyborgs, defend cyborg rights and promote cyborg art. They've donated cyborg antennae to blind communities to help them develop a sense of colour.

Turn over for more AWESOME CYBORGS

4 AWESOME CYBORGS

ROB SPENCE
The man with a camera eye

When Rob Spence lost his eye, he didn't just get a fake one. He created a wireless video camera eye to replace it. It's linked up to a remote receiver and can record everything he sees. It's not connected to his brain or optic nerve, so you might not call him a real cyborg. He has a few different versions, and one of them glows red!

Some people don't like the idea that Rob can film everything and see it as an invasion of their privacy. What do you think?

NEIL HARBISSON
What does red sound like?

The world's first legally recognised cyborg, Neil Harbisson, doesn't see colours – he hears them! Neil was born with extreme colour blindness, or achromatopsia, which affects one in 33,000 people. It means he can only see in black and white.

But now he has a special antenna implanted in his head – his eyeborg. It sticks out like an insect and lets him hear the colours around him, including those beyond the range of human vision! He uses his superpowers to create art and he paints music and speeches by famous people.

His first eyeborg was invented by a cybernetics expert called Adam Montandon. The early version meant Neil had to wear headphones connected to a laptop. But in 2004 he had a chip put inside his skull.

The surgery was rejected by bioethical committees. But it went ahead anyway with the help of a doctor who remains anonymous to this day!

Neil argues that his antenna isn't technology but part of his body. And that's how he persuaded the UK Passport Authority to let him have his eyeborg in his passport photo.

But it doesn't stop there. People can make a phone call straight into his skull. And his friends can send him colours or videos directly into his head. If he's asleep, they can even change the colours of his dreams – woah!

MOON RIBAS
Sensing earthquakes

This cyborg-dancer feels vibrations whenever there's an earthquake on the planet – whatever the time, and wherever it is. She has sensors in her feet that are connected to an online seismograph (an instrument that measures earthquakes).

She uses it for dance performances. She'll stand on stage and wait until an earthquake kicks off. And then her dance will show how it feels. She calls the vibrations her sixth sense.

CAPTAIN CYBORG
The world's first cyborg

In 1998, Kevin Warwick, a Professor of Cybernetics at Reading University, became the world's first cyborg. He had a microchip implanted in his left arm which meant he could open electronic doors automatically and control lights or heaters.

In 2002 he had a much more complex chip implanted directly into his nervous system! It was linked up to a separate robotic arm and was so detailed that when Captain C moved his hand, the robot hand would move in exactly the same way – even though the robotic hand was in the UK and the human hand was in New York!

It's hoped that these amazing achievements will pave the way for treating patients with damaged nervous systems – as well as making humans even more incredible.

INCREDIBLE INSECTS

Robo-bugs to the rescue!

Researchers in Japan have created a remote-controlled, rechargeable cyborg cockroach! Why? Well, they can come to people's rescue in an earthquake. With solar-powered backpacks, they can go into areas that are too dangerous for humans and be controlled remotely.

They've used Madagascar hissing cockroaches as they're big enough to carry the kit and don't have wings that would get in the way.

Robots are already being used to rescue people from collapsed buildings, but robot batteries run out quickly. As well as being solar-powered, these bugs use their own energy to move, so can work for much longer.

Dragonfly drones

Dragonflies are amazing at flying. They can reach up to 48km/h. That's why researchers in the US have turned them into living drones to help rescue people from dangerous areas.

The DragonflEye can be steered up, down, left and right. The dragonfly's steering neurons are genetically modified so that they respond to light. And the dragonflies get a little solar-powered backpack complete with LED lights.

HOW MAY I HELP

Meet the chatbot 'family'

Already nearly 70 years in the making, chatbots were first created as a customer service tool – to answer online questions about something you might be considering buying, for example. Each new generation has become more and more human-like.

ELIZA

BORN: 1966
CREATOR: Joseph Weizenbaum, Massachusetts Institute of Technology

Considered to be the first-ever chatbot, ELIZA recognised key words or phrases and replied by selecting from a bank of pre-programmed responses. Let's say you typed 'Mum bakes the best cookies' on your computer keyboard. ELIZA would pick up the word 'Mum' and ask an open-ended question like 'Tell me more about your family'.

JABBERWACKY

BORN: 1997
CREATOR: Rollo Carpenter, British programmer

This chatbot was invented primarily for entertainment and to replicate 'normal human conversation in an enjoyable, amusing and natural way'. It was helped enormously by the birth of the internet, giving it access to thousands of online human interactions. Several avatars, including 'George' and 'Joan', were offshoots of Jabberwacky, which was rebranded as Cleverbot in 2008.

FAST FACT

Jabberwacky was named after the joyously nonsensical poem 'Jabberwocky', from the Lewis Carroll novel *Through the Looking-Glass*.

YOU?

One goal of AI is to create computer systems that can have a conversation with you. People are already engaging with chatbots – apps that mimic real-life interactions and answer questions – using a combination of AI and NLP (natural language processing)

CHATGPT

BORN 2022
CREATOR Research laboratory OpenAI

ChatGPT is a new chatbot that uses AI to copy and remix data from the internet to answer questions or commands. It's so good at this – users could ask it to write an essay, for example, or explain how algebra works – that some schools have banned it, in case students use it to do their schoolwork for them! The company that created it has also admitted it can get things wrong and give out biased or inappropriate information.

70-90% of customer questions are estimated to be handled by bots by 2024!

8BN The estimated number of voice bots consumers will use globally in 2023

FAST⚡FACT

Just 60 days after its launch, ChatGPT had **100 million users**! It took TikTok nine months to reach the same number.

BETTER TOGETHER

You need to be 18 to use ChatGPT, but why not ask a parent or caregiver if you can explore it together? Here's three things you could ask it to do...

1 Write a play with parts for everyone in your family
2 Create a recipe from the food you have in your cupboard
3 Explain what black holes are, in simple-to-understand terms

ALICE

BORN 1995
CREATOR 'Botmaster' Richard Wallace

ALICE is an acronym for 'Artificial Linguistic Internet Computer Entity'. Building on ELIZA, natural language processing took this chatbot to the next level. She could pick up more 'cues' from a user and, most importantly, ALICE was open source, allowing rival developers to use her as a blueprint for their own chatbots.

Ever wondered why lots of speaking chatbots use a female voice? It's to do with **anthropomorphism**, the human instinct to give objects and creatures human characteristics. Female voices are often seen as being 'warmer and friendlier', so a chatbot with a woman's voice will often strike a human user in the same way.

LOOK, NO HANDS!

Autonomous vehicles drive themselves! Also called driverless or self-driving, they use sensors, cameras, radars and AI to get about. Ready to go for a spin?

TRAINS

Fully-automated train systems run all over the world, including Vancouver, Copenhagen, Paris, Tokyo and Barcelona. They have fewer accidents than when humans operate them. In London, the DLR has been driverless from its opening in 1987.

39.7 million passenger journeys were made on the DLR between 2020–2021

TRUCKS

Head to Toronto, Canada, and you might spot a delivery truck with no driver. A company called Gatik made history by having the first fully driverless delivery trucks in the country.

A driverless truck in action

Safety first

Almost 95% of road accidents are caused by human error. It's thought that autonomous cars could prevent 47,000 serious accidents and save 3,900 lives over the next decade! But there's still work to do to ensure driverless cars are safe on the roads.

Tesla recently launched its 'full self-driving' mode, but there are problems that need fixing: sometimes they mistake the light from the Moon for a yellow traffic light, for example!

PITSTOPS OF THE PAST

1478

Leonardo da Vinci invented a self-propelled cart that could move without being pushed or pulled. Some consider it the world's first driverless car.

1939

General Motors showcased a model of the first self-driving car at the World's Fair. It became a reality in 1958. The car had sensors that helped it drive along a road with wires embedded in it for the car's sensors to pick up.

1961

James Adams created the Stanford Cart. This was the first car to use cameras to autonomously follow a line on the ground.

1977

Japanese researchers at Tsukuba Mechanical designed a driverless car with cameras that could recognise street markings. It reached speeds of nearly 32km/h.

A driverless taxi in China

TAXIS

If you grab a taxi in China, you might wonder why the driver isn't steering! While the taxis are autonomous, there'll still be a safety driver. He won't have his hands on the steering wheel, but will step in if there's an emergency. Recently, completely driverless robo taxis have taken to the streets of Wuhan, but only between 7am and 11pm. San Francisco and downtown Phoenix also have driverless taxis – they're only allowed out at night.

RACE CARS

The Indy Autonomous Challenge pits the world's fastest autonomous race cars against each other. In 2022, PoliMOVE race team smashed the world record for land speed of an autonomous race car. With no driver, just code, their Dallara AV-21 race car reached 309.3km/h!

1995

Carnegie Mellon University researchers took their self-driving car on a 5,000km journey from Pittsburgh to San Diego. The team controlled the speed and braking, but otherwise, the NavLab 5 did its own thing!

2004-2013

The US Defense Advanced Research Projects Agency (DARPA) ran a series of challenges that brought driverless tech on in leaps and bounds. One of them, in 2007, challenged autonomous cars to complete a 96km route within six hours. Four cars completed it.

2015

Tesla launched its autopilot feature, which made cars semi-autonomous. It means cars can drive hands-free on highways in the US.

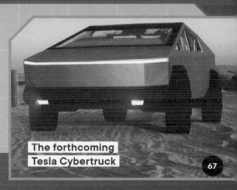

The forthcoming Tesla Cybertruck

THE FEARLESS 10

Robots that go where humans fear to tread...

DANGER!

Robots can replace people when an environment is...

- **HOT** Fighting fire
- **COLD** Sub-zero, icy conditions
- **EXPLOSIVE** Combat zone
- **TOXIC** Contaminated area
- **CONFINED** Place with limited access
- **UNSTABLE** Structure or terrain that might collapse

1 BOMB

PACKBOT carries out bomb disposal in war zones, giving its remote-operator feedback via video, audio and sensors. It's also used to search disaster areas.

2 FIRE

COLOSSUS is a French remote-controlled robot used as a water cannon and for surveillance in situations too dangerous for firefighters. In 2019, Colossus helped put out the fire at Notre-Dame Cathedral in Paris.

3 OIL SPILL

SEASWARM is a system of robots being developed to clean up oil spills by collecting the oil on a nanowire mesh belt. Such spills can cause devastating environmental damage, but scientists estimate 5,000 Seaswarm robots could clean an area the size of the Gulf of Mexico (1.6 million km² of sea!) in a month.

4 COLLAPSED BUILDING

VINE ROBOT is a long, thin, snake-like robot that moves in the same way that a plant grows. When looking for people in a collapsed building it can travel across difficult terrain, climb vertically and carry water or a sensor.

5 ANGRY CATTLE

HOWDY, PARTNER

R2DMOO (not its real name) is an American mobile robot that herds cows. Traditionally, cattle are moved by workers on foot, shouting and waving flags. This can be dangerous and time-consuming. This remote-controlled cowboy eliminates risk and is easily repaired if caught up in a stampede.

6 GLACIER

ICEFIN has swum under the 610 metres of ice beneath the Doomsday Glacier, off the coast of Antarctica. The huge glacier is the size of the US state of Florida and, due to global warming, it's melting. If this glacier collapses the world's sea levels will rise by a foot and it could destabilise other glaciers. Icefin is gathering information that will help scientists predict what will happen.

7 PURSUING POACHERS

AIR SHEPHERD drones are helping in the fight against poaching in South Africa. AI-powered drones watch over the animals day and night and are an effective deterrent to poachers.

8 TSUNAMIS & EARTHQUAKES

SARBOT Is an ROV (Remotely Operated underwater Vehicle), that can dive to depths of 150 metres, film video through dirty water and grab people in need of assistance. SARbot was used to search and assess debris in the wake of Japan's 2011 earthquake and tsunami.

9 SEWAGE PIPES

PIPEBOT is a UK robot being developed to clean Britain's one million kilometres of pipes. An army of Pipebots will inspect water and sewage pipes (full of deadly noxious gases!) for leakages, blockages and signs of wear. It's a dirty job and robots are going to do it.

FACT
Using robots to save lives and collect information helps areas recover from disasters quicker and build defences against future disasters.

10 HURRICANES

HUMMINGBIRD is a drone flown into an area affected by natural disaster to assess damage. It enables engineers and rescuers to see close up what they can't view with binoculars or from satellite images. It was used during the rescue mission in the aftermath of 2005's Hurricane Katrina in the US.

Bridge destroyed by Hurricane Katrina

MIRACLE WORKERS

Robots are revolutionising how the products we use every day are made – and who makes them

A TYPICAL ROBOTIC ARM

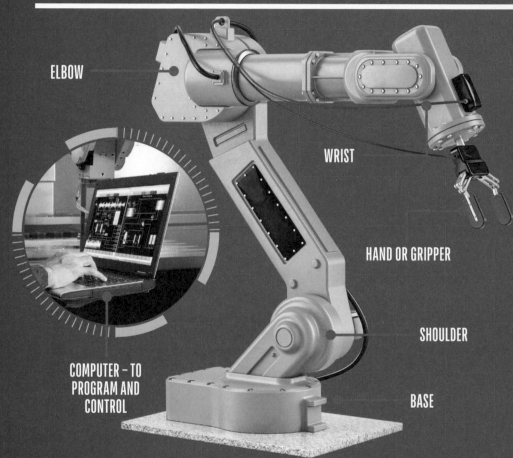

ELBOW

WRIST

HAND OR GRIPPER

SHOULDER

COMPUTER – TO PROGRAM AND CONTROL

BASE

GRIPPING STUFF

Different grippers are used depending on the task

TYPE	FOR
ADAPTIVE / MULTIFINGER	Small, odd-shaped items
TWO- OR THREE-FINGER JAW	Clamping and holding objects steady
MAGNETIC	Smooth metallic surfaces
SOFT AND FLEXIBLE	Made of silicone, they handle delicate products, including food
VACUUM	A cup applies suction to pick up delicate items

2 WAYS TO PROGRAM A ROBOT

1 REMOTE CONTROL

A robot can be controlled by a remote-control device, sometimes known as a teach pendant. It can be connected to the bot via a cable or radio waves, just as we connect to the internet via WiFi. Instructions are stored and repeated as many times as necessary.

2 SHOW ME HOW!

A worker may demonstrate a task or series of tasks to a robot, guiding the arm through the process. The bot memorises the sequence and is then able to repeat it as required.

Built by bots

Car makers use robots throughout the manufacturing process. Among their many tasks they weld parts together, attach door handles and windscreen wipers, construct seats, pick up and place cars on the production line and paint the body. Car paint is toxic to human beings.

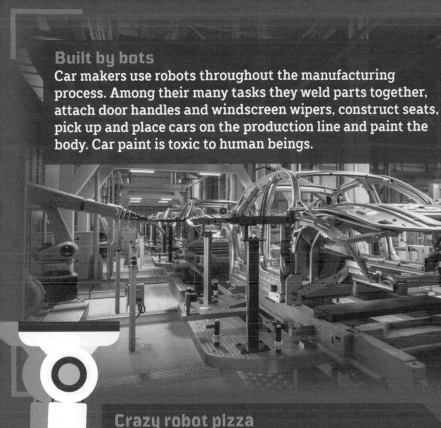

Crazy robot pizza

Pazzi (crazy in Italian) is the 'world's first autonomous restaurant'. Developed in France, this pizza-making robot performs every part of the process, from base to box. It can prepare 10 pizzas at the same time and makes up to 80 pizzas an hour!

OTHER FOOD TASKS ROBOTS CAN DO

PICKING AND PLACING SORTING CUTTING AND SLICING CLEANING PACKAGING DECORATING

Faster fashion

It's only in recent years that industrial robots have been able to handle soft materials. But now, thanks to AI and other advances, they can cut, stitch and knit without help from humans.

The process of stitching a pocket on a shirt usually takes three workers. A robot can do the whole job in just a few seconds. Around 60 million people are currently involved in the manufacture of the world's clothes but that is set to change.

BUILDING THE FUTURE

Robots are big news in the construction industry

BRICKLAYER
The Hadrian X can lay 1,000 bricks in an hour and can build a house in just two days.

PLANNER
Robots can take measurements, draw out detailed plans and check work in progress.

DEMOLITION
Remote-controlled robots can do the dangerous job of taking down entire buildings.

EXCAVATOR
Automated vehicles can take away precise amounts of material from building sites.

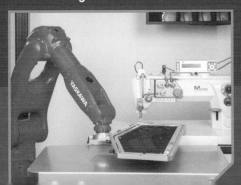

FUTURISTIC FARMING

How robots will help farmers grow crops and care for livestock

Cows

Dairy cows wear wireless collars linked to a computer. As soon as their udders are full, the computer, via the collars, will send the cows to a milking robot. Those robots will analyse the quality of the milk. Trackers in the cows' ears monitor their health, and farmers can follow progress on their smartphones.

Sheep

Instead of using wire fencing that can hurt sheep, shepherds track and contain their flock via GPS collars linked to a smartphone. If a sheep strays beyond the field it is given a small electric shock.

Weeds

A self-driving vehicle travels up and down a field of crops in search of weeds. When one of the vehicle's 13 infrared cameras spots a weed, one of its 65 nozzles sprays herbicide (chemical weed killer). This targeted method can cut use of herbicides by 95%.

Gently does it!

Heavy vehicles like tractors damage soil, making growing crops more difficult. Scientists are developing lighter and cheaper farm vehicles.

Monitoring

Probes in the field and sensors on plants are connected to a phone app that can be used to gauge the crop's health, water intake and the weather.

Drones with infrared cameras assess disease in crops and nutrients in the soil from above.

Drones can also drop pods containing ichneumon wasps over cornfields. The wasps destroy the eggs of European corn borer moths, a widespread pest that eats corn.

Plants grow resistant to herbicides, and chemical weed killer can be toxic to humans. Scientists' goal is for individual weeds to be plucked or blasted out of the ground by a laser.

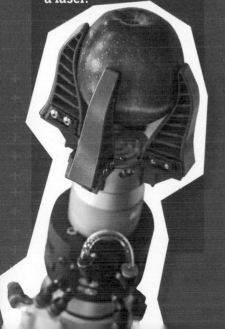

FRUIT

POLLINATION

A robot spots that an apple blossom is open, shoots pollen at it and takes away slow-to-bloom blossom. This allows the tree to use its energy to grow larger apples.

HARVEST

A robot tests how firm and ripe the fruit is. When it's time to harvest, robots pick without damage to the fruit no matter how soft or delicate it may be. A bot can pick two to three fruit per second.

GREENHOUSE

PLANTING

A robot plants 2,400–2,600 cuttings an hour. A human can plant up to 1,400 cuttings per hour.

THINNING

Smaller plants are identified and picked out of the crop, ensuring nutrients go to the bigger, healthier plants.

PEST CONTROL

Small drones search for pesky moths and destroy them with rotating blades.

FAST⚡FACT

A robot in development in Australia can shear a sheep in 5–10 minutes. The world record by a human is 37.9 seconds!

AUSTRALIA

25.69 million people

74.4 million sheep

TO INFINITY AND BEYOND!

Space exploration has developed at warp speed thanks to robots. Unlike humans, machines can survive in hostile environments, don't need to eat, sleep or use the bathroom and can hang out in the galaxy for many years, sending vital information back to Earth. Deep space, here we come...

A roving we will go

Perhaps the most famous space robot of all is the US space agency NASA's Mars rover. These tough robotic vehicles drive across the surface of the Red Planet to help scientists understand what Mars is made of. Some have even sent images of the rocky landscape. There've been five NASA Mars rovers to date. Each one has become more sophisticated and intelligent...

JULY 1997

SOJOURNER

MISSION
To be the first wheeled robot to traverse the Red Planet.

WEIGHT
10.4KG
The same as a medium-sized dog.

JANUARY 2004

SPIRIT & OPPORTUNITY

MISSION
To find evidence of water on Mars.

WEIGHT
170KG EACH
As heavy as a male gorilla.

CURIOSITY

MISSION
To discover if Mars once had the right ingredients to support life.

WEIGHT
899kg
More than a polar bear.

360° Percy can make a full turn on the spot and can tilt 45° in any direction without tipping over.

23 The number of cameras Percy has to gather info about Mars.

FEBRUARY 2021 – TO PRESENT DAY

PERSEVERANCE (aka Percy)

MISSION
To search for past life and find out if humans can survive there.

WEIGHT
1,025kg
As heavy as a black rhinoceros!

Breakthrough
Percy's 2.1m-long robotic arm allowed it to drill deep into Mars's surface and try to find signs of ancient microbial life.

Slow but steady
Percy's top speed is just 0.16km/h, so it wouldn't win in a racing contest, but rovers have to travel at a snail's pace to do their job well.

Turn over for more
ROBOTS IN SPACE

OTHER STAR SPACE ROBOTS

A-PUFFER

Short for: Autonomous Pop-Up Flat Folding
Explorer Robot

MISSION
To scout the Moon to glean information
about hard-to-reach places for astronauts.

MAD SKILLS

Inspired by origami, the
A-PUFFER can flatten
itself down to squeeze
into tight spots like
caves and tunnels.

2.7M The length of
Robonaut 2's legs –
probably double your height!

ROBONAUT 2

MISSION
To help astronauts with lots
of tasks on the International
Space Station.

MAD SKILLS

Although it has yet to take
a spacewalk, the humanoid
robot has over 350 sensors
and has nimble hands to
fix all kinds of things.

150
The number of experts, including scientists and engineers, who built Ginny.

INGENUITY MARS HELICOPTER

Nickname: Ginny

MISSION
Ginny hitched a ride on Perseverance before flying off to take hundreds of images and video footage.

MAD SKILLS
The tiny robotic helicopter is the first vehicle to fly on another planet.

IN THE WORKS
Cutting-edge science and technology mean exciting new space robots are being developed all the time. Here are just a few...

BRUIE
(Buoyant Rover for Under-Ice Exploration)

NASA's robot will be able to collect data from icy bodies in the solar system like Jupiter's moon Europa or Saturn's moon Enceladus. It can roll along the underside of an icy alien ocean and record its chilly view.

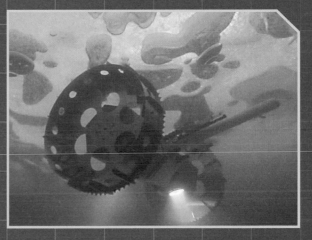

VYOMMITRA
(AKA Space Friend)

Developed by the Indian Space Research Organisation, this 'female' humanoid will be sent into deep space on an uncrewed mission to better understand the effects of weightlessness and radiation on the human body. 'She' can also engage with humans – and mimic them.

ATHLETE
(All-terrain Hex-Legged Extra-Terrestrial Explorer)

Looking a little like a giant spider, this NASA creation is still undergoing testing. It will be able to roll over and 'walk' across challenging terrains on the Moon and Mars, for example. And like an out-of-this-world version of Spider-Man, it will be able to scale vertical rock faces.

SKY-HIGH DRONES

Is it a bird? Is it a plane? No, it's an unmanned aerial vehicle (UAV), or remotely piloted vehicle (RPV). Commonly known as a drone, it's essentially a flying robot! While they can be used for fun, did you know that drones were first developed for military missions?

ACCELEROMETER & ALTIMETER

Speed and direction register via the accelerometer and the altimeter clocks how high the drone is. Working together, they help the UAV land slowly and safely.

120M

The legal height limit for regular, non-military drones in the UK – so they don't get too close to flight paths.

ROTORS

Attached to the motors, the rotors (small propellers) work in different combinations for the drone's movement. For example, hovering happens when two rotors spin clockwise and the other two counterbalance that by spinning anticlockwise.

CONNECTIVITY

Smart devices like phones and tablets or a small hand-held unit controls the path of the drone. GPS and onboard sensors also provide guidance.

CAMERA

Search and rescue missions rely on the drone's camera to scout and find whoever is in trouble – and quickly.

10KM

The maximum altitude achieved by military drones, or over **20 times** the height of the **Empire State Building!**

5G TECHNOLOGY
means drones are becoming **ULTRA-RESPONSIVE,** allowing for high-speed aerial obstacle competitions.

CALL OF DUTY

In theory, the number of soldiers sent to war will decrease as cutting-edge technology is used by the military to create robots that can go into combat. Here are a few examples...

DOGO
It might look cute, but this tiny robot packs a 9-millimetre pistol. DOGO can be controlled remotely to neutralise a kidnapper and save a hostage.

The sky's the limit
There's no getting away from the fact that drones do have a dark side, but they're also used for a whole range of positive things. These include:

- **Monitoring** climate change
- **Search missions** in the wake of natural disasters
- **Delivering goods** (by Amazon, for example)
- **Filming** incredible nature documentaries
- Acting as **'ambulances'** to save lives
- **Dazzling light displays** – remember the epic drone 'show' that illuminated the sky during Buckingham Palace's Platinum Party in 2022?

MAARS
Enemies won't want to mess with this Modular Advanced Armed Robotic System. It's fitted with non-lethal tasers, tear gas and even a grenade launcher.

GUARDBOT
Proving that guns are not always necessary to make a difference in conflict, the small spherical GuardBot was originally designed for a mission to Mars. Today, it's used as a vital 'peaceful' reconnaissance robot. It's equipped with cameras to navigate challenging terrains – snow, sand and water are no match for this tough bot.

DIGITAL DOCTORS

Would you want to be operated on by a robot surgeon? They might look a bit scary, but robots such as this Da Vinci Surgical System allow doctors to operate very precisely using tiny instruments

Robotic surgery

One of the most widely used robots in medicine is the Da Vinci Surgical System – inspired by the famous polymath's study of the human body and his development of automatons.

How robots and AI are used in medicine

- Surgical robots help perform surgery more safely
- Rehabilitation robots and exoskeletons help patients to re-learn movements and build strength after accidents and serious illnesses
- Lab robots perform complex tasks like growing cells in labs, handling dangerous chemicals and analysing data with speed and precision
- Prosthetics and bionics give movement back to people who've had limbs amputated.

How does it work?

The robot has three or four arms. One arm has a camera on the end, two arms act like the surgeon's hands and a fourth arm can be used to remove any blockages the patient might have. The surgeon controls these four arms using a nearby console, and there is a surgical team on hand near the patient so they're always in safe hands.

MEDICAL MILESTONES

1983
Arthrobot, the world's first surgical robot, is used for orthopaedic surgery (treating various bone and muscle injuries).

1985
PUMA 560 (a robotic arm) performs a brain biopsy with 0.05 mm accuracy.

1990
Powered prosthetics are now widely used instead of heavy fixed prosthetics.

1991
SARP (Surgeon Assistant Robot) becomes the first motorised surgical assistant.

1992
Robodoc performs hip and knee replacement surgery.

1998
The ZEUS robotic surgery system performs the first endoscopic (looking inside the body) robotic surgery.

What are the advantages?

The robot uses smaller and more precise incisions than a human can, which means patients need less time to recover from the surgery. They'll also be in less pain after the surgery and smaller cuts means much lower chances of infection.

As the robot that performs the operation is controlled by a surgeon in a separate console, surgeons can also operate on a patient thousands of miles away. This means that patients who need complex surgery could be treated by the most experienced surgeons wherever they are in the world.

CAMERA MONITOR

DA VINCI MEDICAL ROBOT

SURGEON USING CONSOLE

FAST⚡FACT

Since 1999, this amazing piece of kit has performed over 10 million surgeries across the world.

Bionics and prosthetics

Today, when people need to have limbs removed, prosthetic replacements can use a mixture of robotics and AI to achieve amazing outcomes. Rather than a fixed prosthetic that doesn't move, developments in bionic prosthetics have transformed many lives. Bionic prosthetics are programmed to mimic the way a limb works by using biophysics. And the latest technology has even allowed experts to create limbs which are controlled by electrical brain signals, so you just need to think about moving to activate the bionic limb. Wow!

1999

Da Vinci surgical system is approved for use in surgery.

2001

The world's first remote surgery (where the patient and surgeon are in separate locations) is performed using the ZEUS system.

2001

CyberKnife is approved to search and treat tumours anywhere in the body.

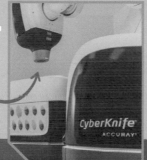

CyberKnife ACCURAY

2010

Rex – a pair of robotic exoskeleton legs that can be used without crutches for support – helps patients with spinal cord injuries build strength and endurance.

NOW

Bionic prosthetic limbs moved with tiny sensors implanted in the brain that interpret electrical signals.

VA-VA-VACUUM!

Hands up if you hate vacuuming, can't stand cleaning or groan when you're asked to help in the garden. Don't worry, there's a whole host of robots that can do your dirty work for you

Vacuum cleaner

Robot vacuum cleaners are small and compact. They don't come with big handles or hoses, because they don't need them. These large, round discs have sensors underneath them, which detect dirt and crumbs on the floor. The sensors then send out signals for the machine to start sucking up any dirt. They're also programmed to avoid obstacles around the home, such as chairs, tables and even humans and pets! Just switch it on and watch the robo-hoover do all the hard work.

Get connected?

All this technology is great for making life a little easier! But some people argue if everything is connected, what happens when a device goes wrong or stops working? Others worry about security risks, especially with programs that can tell whether you're in the house or not.

FAST⚡FACT

As well as vacuum cleaners, you can also get robotic floor mops that will clean your floors.

Smart stuff

Smart devices, such as fridges and ovens, can now connect to the internet to offer extra capabilities. For example, imagine if your fridge could scan its own contents. It would then be able to let you know what food you have and when it will go out of date, or even automatically order items that you're missing, like milk and butter, via the web!

How they work

All smart devices need the following:

1 A sensor to detect input from the world around it.

2 Software to receive the sensory information and make decisions based on the information it has received.

3 An internet connection to send and receive information and data from the many devices around the home.

WINDOW CLEANER

Nowadays there are robots that can stick to windows using special suction pads. With the help of a squeegee mechanism and laser sensors that allow them to navigate, robotic window cleaners will have your glass sparkling in no time. It's just another example of everyday robotic genius.

LAWNMOWER

Just like a robotic vacuum cleaner, a robotic lawnmower can be left to cut the grass unsupervised. These machines have special sensors which tell them when they need to recharge their battery or when it starts raining, so they can make sure to get under cover and stay dry.

VOICE ASSISTANTS

Do you have an Alexa? Or Google assistant? These home assistants work using voice recognition software. Not only can you ask them to play music, but they can control your home's lights and heating.

FAST⚡FACT

Amazon released a cute home robot called Astro in 2022. This small and mobile helper can move objects from one room to another and look out for intruders.

ART ATTACK

The line between human and machine is becoming increasingly blurred with the AI art revolution. Ready to have your mind blown?

Take a GAN-der

A lot of AI art uses Generative Adversarial Networks (GAN), with two types of networks working together to create high-quality images. The first network, the Generator, produces content based on input samples eg the paintings of Vincent Van Gogh. The second network, the Discriminator, tries to identify whether the samples it receives are genuine or ones produced by the Generator. The second network forces the first network to produce more convincing samples that will fool it, while the first network's developing skills force the second network to try harder to spot the 'fakes'. The result: better and better AI-generated artwork.

HOW TO MAKE AI ART...

...without lifting a paint brush!

NAME	WHAT THEY CAN DO
DALL-E, DALL-E 2 (search up surrealist master Salvador Dali) and stable diffusion	• Create near-photorealistic images • Outpainting – stretching and filling in the borders of an already existing image • Blend photography styles via a virtual bridge
GauGAN2 (search for post-impressionist artist Paul Gaugin) combines your sketches and prompts in its AI process	• If you can dream it, GauGAN2 can bring pretty much any vision to life!
MI5.js is an open-source library for machine-learning algorithms	• Give artists, designers and other creatives a crash course in machine learning and its artistic possibilities
Google Deep Dream & **The Next Rembrandt**	• Both capable of producing art that is indistinguishable from that of a human being

WHO (OR WHAT) IS AI-DA?

Masterpieces
Queen Elizabeth II, plus portraits of Billie Eilish, Diana Ross and Kendrick Lamar, made in front of an audience at the Glastonbury Festival in 2022.

Skills
Performance art, paintings, drawings, sculpture and poetry. There's not much she can't do! You can check out 'her' work on insta @aidarobot – she has 120K followers so far! Ai-Da even 'spoke' in front of the British Parliament in 2022, defending the role of technology in the art sphere.

Origins

Ai-Da was created in 2019 by Aidan Meller, a contemporary and modern art specialist, and a team of robotic engineers. She's named after British mathematician Ada Lovelace, celebrated as the first computer programmer back in the 19th century.

$432,500

The amount the algorithm-generated Portrait of Edmond de Belamy, part of a fictional family created by French arts collective Obvious, sold for at auction in 2018.

WORD UP

Can you guess which prompts were used by DALL-E to generate this image? (Answer at the bottom of the page)

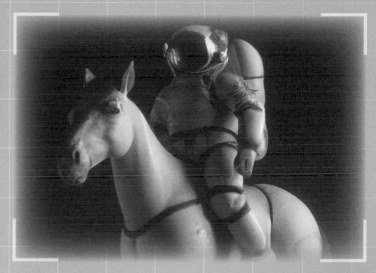

THE BIG DEBATE

AI art is still just getting started and has the potential to make the world more beautiful. But is it 'true' art? Some people believe that art is created for humans, by humans. And way back in the day, it was held that art was the divine (God, for example), working through mankind.

What are your thoughts? Is the writing on the wall for human artists? Or will AI never be able to match the human imagination?

FAKING IT

AI applications can detect art forgeries by cleverly analysing brushstrokes and patterns. Art Recognition, an innovative AI system, made headline news in 2021 when its algorithm returned a 91% probability that the famous Rubens painting *Samson and Delilah* is a fake!

How?

Ai-Da interprets what is in front of her using the cameras in her eyes and computer vision algorithms. A unique control system activates her robotic arms allowing her to paint, draw and even sculpt!

Answer: An astronaut + riding a horse + in a photorealistic style.

85

FUTURE SHOCK

BRIDGING THE UNCANNY VALLEY

The uncanny valley is a phrase for when a humanoid robot appears almost – but not quite – lifelike, and the creepy feeling that this can trigger in human onlookers.

The reasons for this are controversial – some experts believe that humans are hardwired to interpret not-quite 'normal' human behaviour as a sign of contagious illness and to find it unpleasant, which might explain the reaction.

In the next few years, roboticists may be able to construct robots that are truly indistinguishable from flesh-and-blood people, finally bridging the uncanny valley. Being able to produce humanoid robots that don't unnerve regular people will be vital if these mechanical helpers are going to work alongside humans or serve them in businesses, care homes, hospitals and other places where face-to-face interaction is needed.

BUG BUSTERS

Future robots could help to control or even eradicate dangerous diseases by being sent into infected areas to prevent contagions spreading.

The Saul robot has already been used to help aid workers fighting the spread of Ebola in Africa. The robot can remove traces of the virus by firing out pulses of ultraviolet rays. Cool!

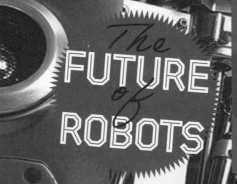

The FUTURE of ROBOTS

A FRIENDLY FACE

Ameca, a robot built by Engineered Arts, is capable of highly realistic facial expressions and answering questions put to it by humans.

Designed to look genderless and friendly, it has been called the most lifelike robot made so far this century. On Christmas Day 2022, Ameca delivered the Alternative Christmas Message on Channel 4. Someday, there might be lots of television programmes presented by intelligent robots!

CYBER SERVANTS

Ever wanted a robot butler that could tidy your room and make you a snack when you're feeling hungry? You're not alone – people have dreamed about (and predicted) the rise of chorebots for decades, but it seems that the reality might finally be edging closer.

In 2021, UBTECH Robotics unveiled Walker X, an in-development robot helper that can wipe down tables, serve drinks, hang up coats and other tasks while avoiding bumping into the furniture. The same year, Samsung gave a demonstration of their own robo-butler, Bot Handy, which can do simple tasks like picking up laundry or loading the dishwasher.

Eco-friendly

One day robots might help to clean up the mess that humans tend to leave behind them, working to reduce pollution of the natural world.

In China, prototype robofish that can gather up microplastics from the ocean are being tested. Eco-bots could also be used to locate and kill invasive species that are destroying ecosystems.

Engineered Arts' Robothespian putting on a show

THAT'S ENTERTAINMENT!

Animatronics have been used in movies and theme park attractions for decades, but more sophisticated versions of performing robots could one day be entertaining large audiences as actors starring in stage shows, musical performances or film and television productions.

Engineered Arts' Robothespian is capable of a range of expressive movements and can be pre-programmed to deliver dialogue and sing songs or controlled remotely by a human so that it can have conversations with audience members. The next few years could see robot actors that are able to create their own performances and interact intelligently with human performers. What's more, these robot performers won't have the physical limitations of humans – they could look like fantastical creatures and perform stunts or routines that are impossible for people.

WE DELIVER

Robot delivery services are already operating around the world and in the future it's likely that all your mail and takeaway orders will be delivered to your door by autonomous vehicles.

A fleet of autonomous delivery robots made by Starship Technologies was launched in Milton Keynes in the UK in 2018. The white, box-shaped, wheeled robots can be loaded up with shopping ordered online and then navigate their way across the city to the customers' homes. The scheme came in handy during the pandemic lockdowns when vulnerable customers struggled to get to shops to buy essentials such as food.

Starship Technologies' delivery robots ready to hit the pavement

SOFT POWER

Up to the present, most robots have been made of hard materials, such as metal, but innovating engineers are currently developing something called soft robotics

SOFT ROBOTICS

What is soft robotics? It's a range of robots made mostly from soft, springy and flexible components, such as polymers (eg rubber), fluids and gels.

How do they work? Rather than being powered by conventional electric batteries, circuits and wires, soft robots function more like biological organisms. Pressurised fluids, triggered by electrical currents, move through the robot, causing different parts of it to contract and expand, mimicking how muscular movements in an animal allow it to travel through an environment. The guiding idea is biomimicry: studying and applying the behaviour and structures of skin and muscles in animals and plants to the design of robots. Soft robots have been built that resemble octopuses, snakes, worms and insects.

ADVANTAGES of SOFT ROBOTS

1 They can be made more cheaply, sometimes by using 3D printing technology.

CHEAPER

2 It's safer for a human to work with a soft robot – if it accidentally hits or collides with a human, it's less likely to cause a serious injury or death.

3 They are more flexible and can collapse or deform when needed, allowing them to squeeze through small gaps and work in tight spaces.

1 DIY ROBOTS

New forms of AI are being developed that can teach themselves and learn from experience. This might mean that in the future AI systems could build and refine new generations of more advanced robots without the need for any human involvement! These machines could outstrip even the wildest ideas or ambitions of human designers. It's also likely that future robots will be able to identify problems with their systems or body parts and repair themselves without the aid of human engineers.

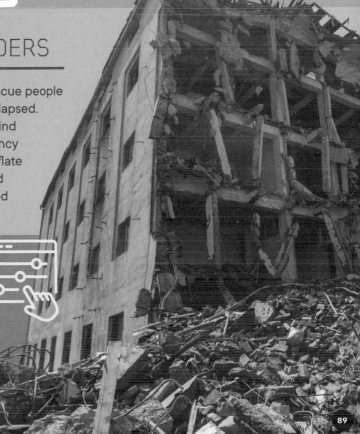

2 OUT ON A LIMB

Soft robotics could also be used to produce prosthetic human limbs that would more closely resemble real arms and legs in their range of movements and appearance.

3 EIGHT-LEGGED WONDERS

Octopus-like soft robots could be used to rescue people from disaster zones where buildings have collapsed. The robot could slither through tiny gaps to find survivors buried under rubble, notify emergency workers of the survivor's location and then inflate to prop up the debris around the survivor and provide an air pocket. They could also be used for exploratory deep-sea missions.

5 They have a greater range of movement: their strength can be quickly adjusted to let them move heavy objects or to manipulate small and delicate objects with precision.

4 They use less energy.

STRENGTH IN NUMBERS

A new branch of engineering – swarm robotics – is changing the way scientists think about robots. Rather than just a single robot performing a task, in the very near future it's possible that whole swarms of robots will work together

SWARM ROBOTICS

What is it? Just like in the animal kingdom, the idea of swarming isn't only about lots of robots doing something at the same time. It's about self-organisation – the way that living things can work together as a group without needing instructions or a leader to solve problems.

EXAMPLE Imagine an ant colony – if you give ants a pile of soil and some time they'll build a complex multi-layered home complete with a sophisticated tunnel network. There's no ant boss telling the others what to do, so how do they know who's doing what and what the end result will look like? Who decides how many floors it'll have? The answers are that they don't, and none of them. Each ant is just following a few simple rules – picking up grains of dirt at a constant rate, dropping them near other grains, choosing grains that other ants have touched. Over time all of these small-scale interactions with the dirt and the other ants add up to the creation of something on a much bigger scale – an ant colony.

KILOBOTS

Kilobots are small, cheap robots that communicate via **infrared signals**. They can form shapes and follow paths.

CELLS

Cells in the body work in much the same way. A cell might not be anything remarkable on its own, but if you take billions of them and they interact following a few simple rules, they come together to form a living organ that's very sophisticated and useful.

INSECT INSIGHT

Inspired by insects' ability to swarm, German robotics company Festo has created delicate eMotion Butterflies and incredible 3D-printed BionicAnts.

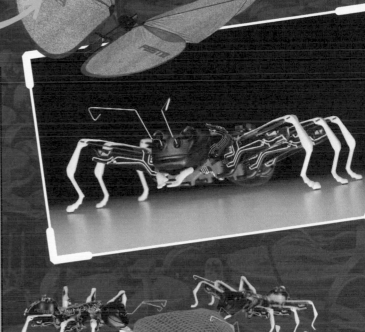

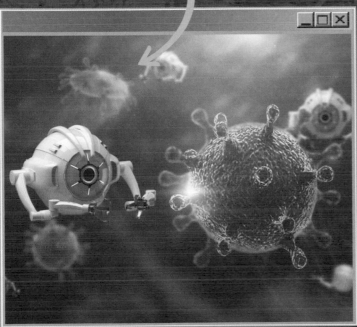

GROUP THINK

Now engineers are thinking about different ways they might use self-organisation in robotics...

1 Swarms of flying robots could monitor crop growth in farming.

2 Swarms of robot builders could construct houses.

3 Nanorobots (really tiny ones) could explore the body looking for cancerous cells.

4 Swarms could even be sent to other planets to search for water and food or gather data.

THE BIG ROBOTS QUIZ

Read the book, then put your newfound knowledge to the test!

1 Who became the world's first cyborg in 1998? (*Turn to p6 for a hint*)

2 What type of AI would be able to think and act just like a human? (*Turn to p8 for a hint*)

3 Who came up with the Chinese room argument? (*Turn to p12 for a hint*)

4 What country granted the robot Sophia citizenship in 2017? (*Turn to p18 for a hint*)

5 Who said that AI is more dangerous than nuclear weapons? (*Turn to p22 for a hint*)

6 In Jewish folklore, what is a golem made from? (*Turn to p28 for a hint*)

7 What automaton did Leonardo Da Vinci invent? (*Turn to p30 for a hint*)

8 Who came up with the Three Laws of Robotics? (*Turn to p32 for a hint*)

9 What was the name of the UK's first robot? (*Turn to p34 for a hint*)

10 Who built the robot tortoises Elmer and Elsie? (*Turn to p36 for a hint*)

11 Unimate was the first what? (*Turn to p38 for a hint*)

12 In what year was Garry Kasparov beaten by the chess computer Deep Blue? (*Turn to p40 for a hint*)

13 What influential 1927 silent film featured one of the earliest onscreen robots? (*Turn to p44 for a hint*)

14 The world's most sophisticated robot dog is called what? (*Turn to p48 for a hint*)

THREE LAWS OF ROBOTICS

ONE
A ROBOT MAY NOT INJURE A HUMAN BEING OR, THROUGH INACTION, ALLOW A HUMAN BEING TO COME TO HARM.

TWO
A ROBOT **MUST OBEY ORDERS GIVEN IT BY HUMAN BEINGS** EXCEPT WHERE SUCH ORDERS WOULD CONFLICT WITH THE FIRST LAW.

THREE
A ROBOT **MUST PROTECT ITS OWN EXISTENCE** AS LONG AS SUCH PROTECTION DOES NOT CONFLICT WITH THE FIRST OR SECOND LAW.

15 What is a cobot?
(*Turn to p50 for a hint*)

16 How tall is the world's biggest robot, Gundam RX-78? (*Turn to p56 for a hint*)

17 What is the world's smallest walking robot? (*Turn to p58 for a hint*)

18 What is the name for an entity with organic and biomechatronic parts? (*Turn to p60 for a hint*)

19 What chatbot was created in 1966? (*Turn to p64 for a hint*)

20 When did Tesla launch its auto-pilot feature in its cars? (*Turn to p66 for a hint*)

21 What robot carries out bomb disposal in war zones? (*Turn to p68 for a hint*)

22 Which Mars rover had the mission of finding out if the planet once had the right ingredients to support life? (*Turn to p74 for a hint*)

23 In what year was the Da Vinci Surgical System approved for use in surgery? (*Turn to p80 for a hint*)

24 How much has Ai-Da's art sold for? (*Turn to p84 for a hint*)

25 What is the name for the creeped-out feeling that lifelike robots can cause in humans? (*Turn to p86 for a hint*)

GLOSSARY

ALGORITHM
A list of rules to follow to complete a task or solve a problem.

ANTHROPOMORPHISM
To give distinctively human characteristics to non-human objects and animals.

APPENDAGE
Something that sticks out from the body, such as a finger, arm, tail or leg.

AUTOMATON
A moving mechanical device that seems to be operating on its own.

AUTONOMOUS
Having the power to make your own decisions.

BIAS
Having thoughts, ideas and beliefs about people, places or things, especially when used to make a judgement or decision.

BIOMIMETICS
The idea that robot engineers take from the movement and behaviour of animals.

CHATBOT
A computer program designed to converse with humans.

COLLABORATIVE
To work together with others.

CYBORG
A being that is part human, part machine.

DATA
Collections of information, especially facts and numbers.

ENTREPRENEUR
Someone who takes a risk to start a business.

GPS
Stands for Global Positioning System, a network of satellites that can pinpoint your position on Earth.

HACKING
Accessing a computer system illegally.

HUMANOID
A machine that looks human.

INFRARED
A type of light that feels warm but cannot be seen by the human eye.

MOTOR
A rotating machine that transforms electrical power into movement.

NANOBOT
A very small robot.

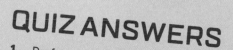

NATURAL LANGUAGE PROCESSING
The ability of a computer program to understand human language.

PROTOTYPE
An early model of a machine or product.

RADAR
A system that uses radio waves to locate and track objects.

REGENERATIVE
Able to heal, regrow or be restored after being damaged or inactive.

ROBOTICIST
A scientist who designs, builds and programs robots.

ROVER
A robot used to explore other planets.

SENSOR
A device that detects changes in its environment, such as light or heat.

SURVEILLANCE
Closely watching a person or place.

QUIZ ANSWERS

1. Professor Kevin Warwick
2. Strong or general AI
3. John Searle
4. Saudi Arabia
5. Elon Musk
6. Clay
7. A mechanical knight
8. Isaac Asimov
9. Eric
10. William Grey Walter
11. Industrial robot
12. 1997
13. Metropolis
14. Spot
15. A collaborative robot
16. 18 metres
17. Microrobot crab
18. Cyborg
19. Eliza
20. 2015
21. Packbot
22. Curiosity
23. 1999
24. More than $1 million
25. The Uncanny Valley

INDEX

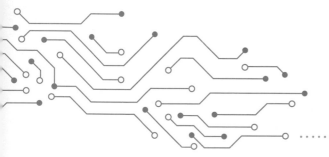

First published 2023 by Button Books, an imprint of Guild of Master Craftsman Publications Ltd, Castle Place, 166 High Street, Lewes, East Sussex, BN7 1XU, UK. Copyright in the Work © GMC Publications Ltd, 2023. ISBN 978 1 78708 148 2. Distributed by Publishers Group West in the United States. All rights reserved. No part of this publication may be reproduced, stored in a retrieval system, or transmitted in any form or by any means without the prior permission of the publisher and copyright owner. While every effort has been made to obtain permission from the copyright holders for all material used in this book, the publishers will be pleased to hear from anyone who has not been appropriately acknowledged and to make the correction in future reprints. The publishers and authors can accept no legal responsibility for any consequences arising from the application of information, advice, or instructions given in this publication. A catalogue record for this book is available from the British Library. Editorial: Susie Duff, Nick Pierce, Rachel Roberts, Robert Hiley, Mary Wessel, Claire McKinson, Lorna Cowan. Design: Tim Lambert, Jo Chapman, Emily Hurlock, Isobel Lundie, Dean Chillmaid, Jonathan Bacon. Publisher: Jonathan Grogan. Production: Jim Bulley. Photos: Shutterstock.com Illustrations: Michelle Urra, Sara Thielker, Alex Bailey. Colour origination by GMC Reprographics. Printed and bound in China.

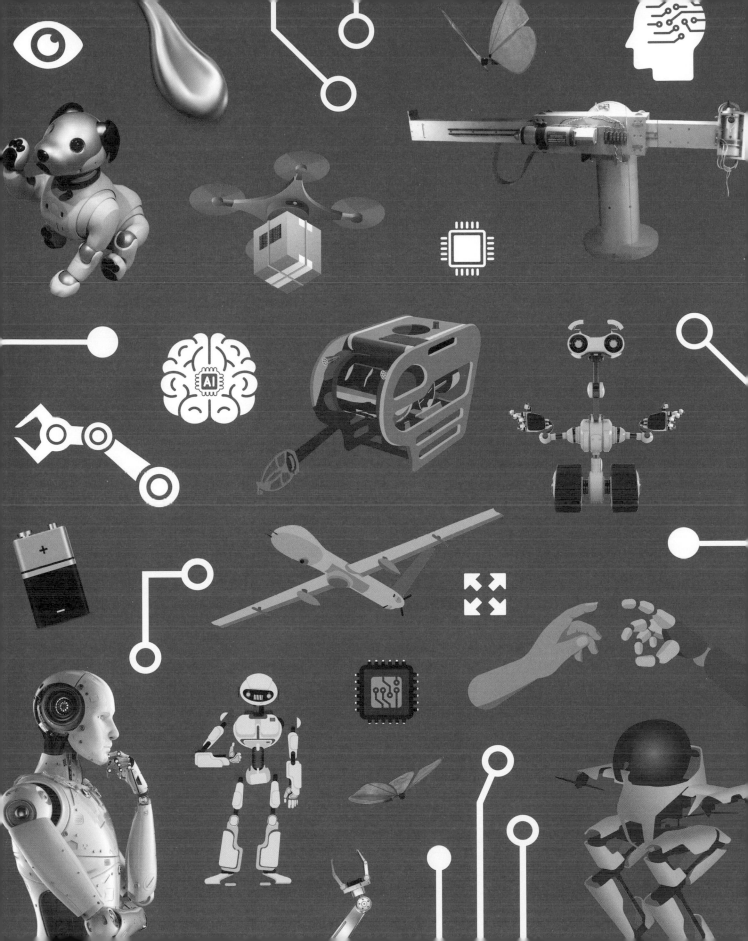